RECOLLECTIONS AND IMPRESSIONS

OF

JAMES A. McNEILL WHISTLER

Whistler (From a Sketch by Rajon)

RECOLLECTIONS AND IMPRESSIONS

OF

JAMES A. MCNEILL WHISTLER

BY

ARTHUR JEROME EDDY

AUTHOR OF " DELIGHT : THE
SOUL OF ART," ETC.

BENJAMIN BLOM, INC.
Publishers New York 1972

Second Edition
First published Philadelphia, 1904
Reissued 1972 by
Benjamin Blom, Inc.
New York, N.Y. 10025

Library of Congress
Catalog Card Number 71-173163

Printed in the
United States of America

To L. O. E.

This Sixteenth Day of September
Nineteen Hundred and Three

FOREWORD

Most of what is contained herein has been collected from time to time within the past ten years and jotted down for use in certain lectures on Whistler and his art. The lectures were, as is this book, a tribute to the great painter.

The reminiscences are mostly personal. Many of the anecdotes—though perhaps equally familiar to others—were had from the artist's own lips. The views concerning his art, whether right or wrong, were formed while watching him at work day after day, and after many interviews in which, now and then, he would speak plainly concerning art. At the same time not so much as a thought must be attributed to him unless expressly quoted.

The biographical data—just sufficient to furnish a connecting thread and aid in the appreciation—have been gathered from casual sources, and are, no doubt, subject to incidental corrections.

Only when a duly authorized "life and letters" is published by those who have access to the material that must exist will the great artist be known by the world as he really was—a profoundly earnest, serious, loving, and lovable man.

Meanwhile, those who believe in his art must— like the writer—speak their convictions for what they are worth.

CONTENTS

❧

I

CONTENTS

ILLUSTRATIONS

" This man, who took no joy in the ways of his brethren —who cared not for conquest, and fretted in the field—this designer of quaint patterns—this deviser of the beautiful— who perceived in Nature about him curious curvings, as faces are seen in the fire—this dreamer apart, was the first artist."—WHISTLER'S "Ten o'Clock."

RECOLLECTIONS AND IMPRESSIONS

OF

JAMES A. McNEILL WHISTLER

I

Why he never Returned to America—Tariff on Art—South America—Valparaiso.

Now that the end has come and the master is no more, the scattered sheaves of stories and anecdotes, of facts and fancies, of recollections and impressions may be gathered together from the four quarters, and the story of his work be told,—not in detail, not in sequence, for some one will write his life, but in fragmentary fashion as the thoughts occur.

For the better part of his life Whistler fought the prejudices of all Europe and of his own country.

He once said, with a tinge of bitterness in his tone :

"The papers in America seem content to publish second-hand whatever they find about me in English journals that is mean and vindictive or that savors of ridicule. Aside from the hopeless want of originality displayed in echoing the stupidities of others, what has become of that boasted love of fair play?

RECOLLECTIONS AND IMPRESSIONS

Even the phlegmatic Englishman takes the part of a fellow-countryman against many—quite regardless; but the American press—bully like—leans to the side of the bully and weakly cries, bravo! whenever the snarling pack on this side snaps at the heels of an American who mocks them at the doors of their own kennels.

"One would think the American people would back a countryman—right or wrong—who is fighting against odds; but for thirty years they laughed when the English laughed, sneered when they sneered, scoffed when they scoffed, lied when they lied, until,—well, until it has been necessary to reduce both nations to submission."

For a time he worked without a word, then:

"But when France—in all things discerning—proclaimed the truth, America—still blind—hastened to shout that she, too, saw the light, and poured forth adulation *ad nauseam.*"

"But would you say that Americans are as dense as the English?"

"Heaven forbid that the Englishman's one undeniable superiority be challenged; but an Englishman is so honest in his stupidity that one loves him for the—virtue; whereas the American is a 'smart Aleck' in his ignorance, and therefore intolerable."

But that was years ago, when the unconverted were more numerous on this side,—there are still a number of stubborn dissenters, but in the chorus of praise their voices are scarce more than a few discordant notes.

OF JAMES A. McNEILL WHISTLER

Of late Whistler had but little cause to complain of lack of appreciation on this side,—for, while an art so subtle as his is bound to be more or less misunderstood, critics, amateurs, and a goodly portion of the public have for a long time acknowledged his greatness as an etcher, a lithographer, and a painter. In fact, for at least ten years past his works have been gradually coming to this country—where they belong. England and Scotland have been searched for prints and paintings until the great collections— much greater than the public know—of his works are here. Some day the American people will be made more fully acquainted with the beautiful things he has done, many of which have never been seen save by a few intimate friends.

The struggle for recognition was long and bitter, —so long and so bitter that it developed in him the habits of controversy and whimsical irritability by which he was for a generation more widely known than through his art.

When it was once reported that he was going to America, he said, "It has been suggested many times ; but, you see, I find art so absolutely irritating to the people that, really, I hesitate before exasperating another nation."

To another who asked him when he was coming, he answered, with emphasis, "When the duty on art is removed."

The duty on art was a source of constant irritation to Whistler,—for, while the works of American artists residing abroad are admitted free, the artist is compelled to make oaths, invoices, and take out consular certificates, and pay the consular fees in line with the shipper of olive oil and cheese.

There was even a time, under the present law, when the works of American painters were not admitted free. The law reads, the works of American artists "residing *temporarily* abroad" shall be admitted free, etc.

Some department at Washington made an off-hand ruling that if an American artist had resided more than five years abroad his works would be subject to duty as those of a foreigner, thereby expatriating with a stroke of the pen four-fifths of the Americans who are working like dogs—but as artists—to make the world beautiful.

To Whistler, Sargent, and the many prosperous ones the ruling did not greatly matter, but to the younger men who could not earn money enough to get home it did matter, and for a time it looked as if American art in Europe would be obliterated,—for American art in Europe depends for its support and aggressiveness on the American artists over there. Drive these men home, or expatriate them, so as to compel them to cast their lots with France, or England, or Italy, and what would become of those American sections in foreign exhibitions which for at least a dozen years past have commanded the serious consideration of all thoughtful observers as containing elements of strength, sobriety, and promise found nowhere else in the entire world of art?

OF JAMES A. McNEILL WHISTLER

Happily an appeal to the Secretary of the Treasury—a man interested in art—resulted in an immediate reversal of the ruling, and the works of American artists come in free unless the artist declares his intention of residing abroad permanently.

But while the ban on American painting is lifted, sculpture is in a bad way. Under the law only sculpture "wrought by hand" from marble or metal by the sculptor is to be classed as art. Inasmuch as the sculptor never did work bronze by hand, and nowadays very rarely touches the marble, there is no sculpture which comes within the law. The federal courts of New York, high and low, have soberly held that unless it is shown that bronzes are "wrought by hand" by the sculptor, instead of cast from plaster, which in turn is made from the clay, they are commercial products and classed with bronze cooking utensils at forty-five per cent. duty. However, a federal judge in Chicago, somewhat more familiar with art processes, has held that the New York decisions are arrant nonsense, and original bronzes by Rodin, St. Gaudens, and other sculptors, made in the only known way of producing bronzes, should be classed as art. What other federal courts may hold—each, under our wonderful system, having the right to its opinion until the Supreme Court is called upon to finally end the differences—Heaven alone knows ; but for the present it behooves lovers of art to bring in their original bronzes and marbles by way of Chicago.

These were some of the things Whistler—in

common with many an ordinary man—could not understand.

A few years ago an effort was made to have an exhibition of his pictures in Boston. He was appealed to, but refused :

"God bless me, why should you hold an exhibition of pictures in America? The people do not care for art."

"How do you know? You have not been there for many years."

"How do I know! Why, haven't you a law to keep out pictures and statues? Is it not in black and white that the works of the great masters must not enter America, that they are not wanted——"

"But——"

"There are no 'buts' about it except the fool who butts his head against the barrier you have erected. A people that tolerates such a law has no love for art,—their protestation is mere pretence."

That a great nation should deliberately discourage the importation of beautiful things, should wallow in the mire of ugliness and refuse to be cleansed by art, was to him a mystery,—for what difference does it make whether painting, poetry, and music come out of the East or out of the West, so long as they add to the happiness of a people? And why should painting and sculpture find the gate closed when poetry and music are admitted?

He did not know the petty commercial considerations which control certain of the painters and

sculptors and some of the institutions supposed to
be devoted to art.

For is not art the most " infant" of all the " infant
industries" of this great commercial nation ?   And
should not the brush-worker at home be given his
meed of protection against the pauper brush-workers
of Europe—even against Rembrandt and Velasquez
and all the glorious Italians ?

Beethoven and Mendelssohn and Mozart, Shakespeare and Milton,—their works, even their original
manuscripts, if in existence, though costly beyond
many paintings, come in without let or hinderance ;
but the work of the painter, the original manuscript
of the poet in line, of the composer of harmonies
in color, may not cross the border without tribute.

A symphony in sound is welcomed ; a symphony
in color is rejected.   Why this discrimination in
favor of the ear and against the eye ?

There is no reason, but an inordinate amount of
selfishness, in it all.   The wire-pulling painter at
home, backed up by the commercially-managed art
institution, makes himself felt in the chambers at
Washington where tariffs are arranged, and painting and sculpture are removed from the free list and
placed among the pots and kettles of commerce.

Where is the poet and where is the musician in
this distribution of advantages ?   Why should American poetry and American music be left to compete
with the whole world while American painting and
American sculpture are suitably encouraged by a
tariff of twenty per cent. ?—a figure fixed, no doubt,

RECOLLECTIONS AND IMPRESSIONS

as is the plea, to make good the difference in wages,
—pauper labor of Europe,—pauper artists.   Alas!
too true ; shut the vagabonds out that their aristo-
cratic American confrères residing at home may
maintain their "standard of living."

Of all the peoples on the face of the globe, high
and low, civilized and savage, there is just one that
discourages the importation of the beautiful, and that
one happens to be the youngest and the richest of
all—the one most in need of what it wilfully ex-
cludes.

Notwithstanding all these reasons for not coming,
he had a great desire to visit this country, and in
letters to friends on this side he would again and
again express his firm intention to come the following summer or winter, as the season might be.   The
death of Mrs. Whistler, some six years ago, and his
own ill health prevented,—but there was no lack of
desire.

Strangely enough, he did take a sailing-ship for
South America, away back in the sixties, and while
there painted the "Crepuscule in Flesh Color and
Green ; Valparaiso" and the "Nocturne Blue and
Gold ; Valparaiso."

Speaking of the voyage, he said :

"I went out in a slow sailing-ship, the only passenger.
During the voyage I made quite a number of sketches and
painted one or two sea-views,—pretty good things I thought
at the time.   Arriving in port, I gave them to the purser to

22

Crepuscule in Flesh Color and Green; Valparaiso

take back to England for me. On my return, some time later, I did not find the package, and made inquiries for the purser. He had changed ships and disappeared entirely. Many years passed, when one day a friend, visiting my studio, said :

" ' By the way, I saw some marines by you in the oddest place you can imagine.'

" ' Where?' I asked, amazed.

" ' I happened in the room of an old fellow who had once been a purser on a South American ship, and while talking with him saw tacked up on the wall several sketches which I recognized as yours. I looked at them closely, and asked the fellow where he got them.

" ' " Oh, these things," he said ; " why, a chap who went out with us once painted them on board, off-hand like, and gave them to me. Don't amount to much, do they?"

" ' " Why, man, they are by Whistler."

" ' " Whistler," he said, blankly. " Who's Whistler?"

" ' " Why, Whistler the artist,—the great painter."

" ' " Whistler, Whistler. I believe that was his name. But that chap warn't no painter. He was just a swell who went out with the captain ; he thought he could paint some, and gave me those things when we got to Valparaiso. No, I don't care to let them go,—for, somehow or other, they look more like the sea than real pictures." ' "

Whistler made several attempts to find these sketches, but without success.

As illustrating his facility of execution when time pressed, he painted the " Crepuscule in Flesh Color and Green," which is a large canvas and one of his best things, at a single sitting, having prepared his colors in advance of the chosen hour.

He could paint with the greatest rapidity when out-of-doors and it was important to catch certain effects of light and color.

RECOLLECTIONS AND IMPRESSIONS

In 1894 he exhibited in Paris three small marines which were marvels of clearness, force, and precision ; he had painted them in a few hours while in a small boat, which the boatman steadied against the waves as best he could. He placed the canvas against the seat in front of him and worked away direct from nature.

II

A Family of Soldiers—Grandfather founded Chicago—Birth—St. Petersburg—West Point—Coast Survey—His Military Spirit.

He came of a race of fighters. The family is found towards the end of the fifteenth century in Oxfordshire, at Goring and Whitechurch on the Thames ; one branch was connected with the Websters of Battle-Abbey, and descendants still live in the vicinity ; another branch is in Essex, and from this sprang Dr. Daniel Whistler, President of the College of Physicians in London in the time of Charles the Second, and described as "a quaint gentleman of rare humor," and frequently mentioned in " Pepys's Diary."

From the Oxfordshire branch, one Ralph, a son of Hugh Whistler of Goring, went to Ireland and founded the Irish branch from which sprang Major John Whistler, the first representative of the family in America, and grandfather of the painter.

Major Whistler was a British soldier under Burgoyne, and was taken prisoner at the battle of Saratoga. At the close of the war he returned to England and made a runaway match with the daughter of a Sir Edward Bishop.

Returning to this country with his wife, he settled at Hagerstown, Maryland, and soon after enlisted in the American army.

"He was made a sergeant-major in a regiment that was called 'the infantry regiment.' Afterwards he was adjutant of Garther's regiment of the levies of 1791, which brought him into General St. Clair's command. He was severely wounded November 4, 1791, in a battle with the Indians on the Miami River. In 1792 'the regiment of infantry' was, by Act of Congress, designated as the 'First Regiment,' and to this John Whistler was assigned as first lieutenant. In November, 1796, he was promoted to the adjutancy, and in July, 1797, he was commissioned a captain."

While captain of the "First Regiment," then stationed at Detroit, he was, in 1803, ordered to proceed to the present site of the city of Chicago and construct Fort Dearborn.

He and his command arrived on August 17, at two o'clock in the afternoon, and at once staked out the ground and began the erection of palisades for protection against the Indians.

The captain had with him at the time one son, William, who was a lieutenant in the army, and who was commander of Fort Dearborn in 1833, when the fort was finally abandoned as a military post. Another son, John, remained in the East.

On the completion of the fort the captain brought out the remaining members of his family,—his wife, five daughters, and his third son, George, then but three years old, and afterwards the father of the artist.

"The daughters were Sarah, who married James Abbott, of Detroit,—the ceremony took place in the fort, shortly after the family came ; the wedding-trip was made to Detroit on horseback, over an Indian trail and the old territorial road ; they had two nights of camping out ; their effects were carried on pack-horses,—Ann, married Major Marsh, of the army ; Catherine, married Major Hamilton, of the army ; Harriet, married Captain Phelan, also of the army ; Caroline—eight months old when her father built Fort Dearborn—was married in Detroit, in 1840, to William R. Wood, of Sandwich, Georgia."

When the army was reduced in June, 1815, Major Whistler was retired, and in 1818 appointed military storekeeper at Jefferson Barracks, St. Louis. He died at Bellefontaine, Missouri, in 1827. "He was a brave officer and became the progenitor of a line of brave and efficient soldiers."

To a visitor from Chicago the artist once said :

"Chicago, dear me, what a wonderful place ! I really ought to visit it some day,—for, you know, my grandfather founded the city and my uncle was the last commander of Fort Dearborn."

George Washington Whistler, the father of the painter, became an engineer of great reputation, rose to the rank of major, and in 1842 accepted the invitation of Czar Nicholas to superintend the construction of the St. Petersburg and Moscow Railroad, and it is said that, with the exception of John Quincy Adams, no American in Russia was held in such high estimation.

Major Whistler has been described as a very handsome man ; he had rather long curling hair which framed a most agreeable face. " He might have been taken for an artist, rather than for a military engineer. Yet he was, in every sense, a manly man, with most attractive expression and ways."

Whistler's mother—his father's second wife—was Anna Mathilda McNeill, a daughter of Dr. C. D. McNeill, of Wilmington, North Carolina.

So much for the stock from which Whistler sprang, a line of able men and good fighters. In a round-about way he must have inherited some of the traits of that " quaint gentleman of rare humor" so frequently mentioned by garrulous Samuel Pepys, who says in one place, " Dr. Whistler told a pretty story. . . . Their discourse was very fine ; and if I should be put out of my office, I do take great content in the liberty I shall be at of frequenting these gentlemen's company."

It is reported that Whistler once stated he was born in St. Petersburg, and he certainly seemed to take delight in mystifying people as to the date and place of his birth,—part of his habitual indifference to the sober requirements of those solemn meta-physical entities Time and Space.

One friend has insisted in print upon Baltimore

as his birthplace, another upon Stonington, Connecticut.

His model once asked him :

" Where were you born ?"

" I never was born, my child ; I came from on high."

Quite unabashed, the model retorted :

" Now, that shows how easily we deceive ourselves in this world, for I should say you came from below."

The Salon catalogue of 1882 referred to him as " McNeill Whistler, born in the United States."

His aversion to discussing dates, the lapse of years, the time it would take to paint a portrait, or do anything else, amounted to a superstition.

For him time did not exist. He did not carry a watch, and no obtrusive clock was to be seen or heard anywhere about him. He did not believe in mechanical devices for nagging and prompting muchgoaded humanity. If he were invited to dinner, it was always the better part of wisdom to order the dinner at least a half-hour later than the moment named in the invitation.

He once had an engagement to dine with some distinguished people in a distant part of London. A friend who wished to be on time was waiting for him in the studio. It was growing late, but Whistler kept on painting, more and more absorbed.

" My dear fellow," his friend urged at last, " it is frightfully late, and you have to dine with Lady ——. Don't you think you'd better stop ?"

"Stop?" fairly shrieked Whistler. "Stop, when everything is going so beautifully? Go and stuff myself with food when I can paint like this? Never! Never! Besides, they won't do anything until I get there,—they never do!"

An official connected with an international art exhibition was about to visit Paris to consult with the artists. To save time, he sent notes ahead making appointments at his hotel with the different men at different hours. To Whistler he sent a note fixing a day at "4.30 precisely," whereupon Whistler regretfully replied:

"DEAR SIR: I have received your letter announcing that you will arrive in Paris on the —th. I congratulate you. I never have been able, and never shall be able, to be anywhere at '4.30 precisely.'
"Yours most faithfully,
"J. McN. WHISTLER."

To the stereotyped inquiry of the sitter:

"About how many sittings do you require, Mr. Whistler?"

"Dear me, how can I tell? Perhaps one, perhaps—more."

"But—can't you give me some idea, so I can arrange——"

"Bless me, but you must not permit the doing of so trivial a thing as a portrait to interfere with the important affairs of life. We will just paint in those odd moments when you have nothing better to do."

OF JAMES A. McNEILL WHISTLER

"Suppose I am compelled to leave the city before it is finished?"

"You will return next summer, and we will resume where we left off, as the continued-story-teller says."

And no amount of persuasion could get him to say when he expected to finish a work.

He would frequently say :

"We will just go ahead as if there were one long holiday before us, without thinking of the end, and some day, when we least expect it, the picture is finished ; but if we keep thinking of the hours instead of the work, it may never come to an end."

This indifference to time kept him young—to the very last. He persistently refused to note the flight of years.

There was once a very old Indian, how old no one knew, in Northern Michigan who, when asked his age by the pertinaciously curious, always replied, "I do not count the years ; white people do—and die."

His father went to Lowell, Massachusetts, in 1834 to take charge of the construction of the canals and locks. He resided in a house on Worthen Street, and there Whistler was born on July 10.

In a history of Lowell it is stated that Whistler was probably born in what was known as the Paul Moody house, a fine old house which stood on the site of the present city hall ; but quite possibly the family occupied a house owned by the proprietors

31

of the locks and canals, which still stands and is pointed out as the "Locks and Canal house."

The old parish book of St. Anne's Episcopal Church contains the following entry under 1834 :

" Nov. 9, Baptized James Abbott, infant son of George Washington and Anna Mathilda Whistler. Sponsors, the parents.   T. Edson."

Rev. Theodore Edson was the rector of the church.

The adoption of his mother's maiden name, McNeill, as part of his own was apparently an after-thought.

He had two brothers, William and Kirke, a half-brother, George, and a half-sister, Deborah, who married Seymour Haden, the well-known physician and etcher, who figures in "Gentle Art" as the "Surgeon-etcher."   Of the brothers, Kirke died young, George remained in this country, William became a well-known physician in London, dying a few years ago.

The family afterwards spent a short time in Stonington, where Major Whistler had charge of the construction of the railroad to Providence.   They used to drive to church in Westerly in a chaise fitted with railway wheels, so as to travel on the tracks. There were no Sunday trains in those days, so the track was clear.   An ingenious device enabled the horse to cross the culverts.

A locomotive named "Whistler" after the distinguished engineer—a felicitous name—was in use until comparatively few years ago.

OF JAMES A. McNEILL WHISTLER

In the spring of 1840 Major Whistler was appointed consulting engineer for the Western Railroad, running from Springfield to Albany, and the family moved to Springfield and lived in what "is now known as Ethan Chapin homestead, on Chestnut Street, north of Edwards Street."

Old residents of the vicinity claim to remember "well the curly locks and bright, animated countenance of the boy," and that the three boys "were always full of mischief,"—not an uncommon trait in youngsters, probably still less uncommon in Whistlers.

Shortly after the railroad to Albany was opened a wreck occurred, and a niece of Major Whistler, who was on her way to visit him, was badly injured. She was taken to his house, and it was a long time before she recovered.

The accident made a strong impression on Whistler, and possibly accounts for some of the dislike he often showed towards travelling alone. It was only in crossing crowded streets and in the confusion and bustle of travel that he showed what might be called nervousness.

With characteristic gallantry he would offer a lady his arm to aid her in crossing the Strand or the Boulevard, but he made sure of the places of refuge and took no chances ; if in a hurry, she would better cross alone.

Once, not many years ago, he was at Dieppe, and wrote a friend in Paris almost daily that he would be in the city to see him. A week passed, and the friend, fearing he would be obliged to leave without seeing Whistler, wrote him he would come to Dieppe and see the work he was doing there, to which sug-gestion Whistler replied most cordially by wire.

The friend packed and went, expecting to stay a night or two at least ; but, lo ! Whistler, bag in hand, met him in the village to take the next train back ; whereupon the friend, much surprised, said :

" If you intended going to Paris to-day, why under the sun did you let me ride half a day to get here ?"

"Well, you see, I don't like to travel alone ; happy thought yours to come down after me."

And back they went, after a delightful luncheon in that little old restaurant near the cathedral, where there is an ancient stone trough filled with water for cooling and cleaning vegetables. The luncheon, the way it was ordered, and the running fire of comment and directions by Whistler to the stout old woman who did it all, were worth the journey to Dieppe.

Whistler will be mourned more by these lowly people who used to serve him with pleasure, because he took such a vital interest in what they did, than by many who own his works.

A diary kept by the artist's mother contains this entry, under date of July 10, 1844 :

"A poem selected by my darling Jamie, and put under my plate at the breakfast-table, as a surprise on his tenth birthday."

The little poem of twelve lines was addressed

"To My Mother," and subscribed "Your Little James."

When the boy was eleven years old, Sir William Allen, a Scotch painter, visited the family. Mrs. Whistler's diary contains the following entry :

"The chat then turned upon the subject of Sir William Allen's painting of Peter the Great teaching the majiks to make ships. This made Jimmie's eyes express so much interest that his love for the art was discovered, and Sir William must needs see his attempts. When my boys had said good-night, the great artist remarked to me, 'Your little boy has uncommon genius, but do not urge him beyond his inclination.' I told him his gift had only been cultivated as an amusement, and that I was obliged to interfere, or his application would confine him more than we approved."

The diary records the same year a visit to the old palace at Peterhoff, where "our Jimmie was so saucy as to laugh" at Peter's own paintings.

When Major Whistler first went to Russia he left "Jamie" for a time in Stonington with his aunt, and the two older children, George and Deborah, in England.

After the death of Major Whistler, in St. Petersburg, in 1849, the wife and children returned to this country, and lived for a time in Connecticut.

Whistler wished to enter West Point, and he persuaded his half-brother to write Daniel Webster, to enlist his sympathy. The letter was dated February 19, 1851. It referred to the father's career and services and asked that James be appointed to the Academy.

He was appointed by President Fillmore, and entered July 1, 1851, registering from Pomfret, Windham County, Connecticut, where his mother was then living.

Whistler was so small in stature and physique that it is surprising he was received ; the military record of his family was no doubt the controlling considera-tion.

He possessed all the pugnacity and courage re-quired for a soldier, and the military spirit was strong in him, yet such was his bent towards art that his career at the Academy was not one of glory ; but he became very popular with his comrades and proba-bly led in all their mischievous pranks.

The official records show that at the end of the first year, in 1852, he stood forty-one in a class of fifty-two,—his standing in the different studies being as follows : Mathematics 47, English studies 51, French 9. At the end of his second year he stood number one in drawing, but was not examined in other studies, being absent with leave on account of ill health. In 1854 his standing was as follows : Philosophy 39, Drawing 1, Chemistry deficient. For his deficiency in chemistry he was discharged from the Academy on June 16, 1854.

A lady once asked him why he left the Academy, and he replied :

" If silicon had been a gas, madame, I should have been a soldier."

OF JAMES A. McNEILL WHISTLER

On leaving West Point he took it into his head that Fate had intended him for a sailor, and he tried to enter the Naval Academy at Annapolis, but he could not get the appointment.

Through an old friend of the family, Captain Benham, of the Coast and Geodetic Survey, he was employed as draughtsman in that department in Washington from November 7, 1854, to February 12, 1855, at one dollar and a half a day. In these days he signed himself James A. Whistler. His lodgings were in an old house still standing on the northeast corner of E and Twelfth Streets. He was always late to breakfast, and scribbled pictures on the unpapered walls. When the landlord objected, he said :

" Now, now, never mind ; I'll not charge you anything for the decoration."

Neither time nor the rules of the department had any terrors for him. Even in those early days he was a law unto himself. In one instance the following entry appears against his name :

"Two days absent and two days deducted from monthly pay for time lost by coming late to office."

To correct these dilatory habits Captain Benham conceived the brilliant idea of having a fellow-clerk of punctual habits call each morning for Whistler and bring him to the office on time. The captain believed that the example and influence of a more methodical companion would reform the erring one and get him to the office at nine o'clock ; but it turned out quite otherwise, for Whistler proved so charming a host each morning that both were late.

At the end of a week the mentor reported that his efforts were wasted and unless relieved he, too, would acquire the obnoxious habit, for each morning Whistler managed to so interest him in the mysteries of coffee-making and the advantages of late breakfasts that it was impossible to get away.

Of him and his habits in those days a fellow-draughtsman,[1] who is still in the service, says :

" He was about one year younger than myself, and therefore about twenty years old at that time. He stayed but a little over three months, and I have not met him since, but retain a more vivid recollection of his sojourn than of that of many other draughtsmen who succeeded him and remained much longer. This may be partly for the reason that Captain Benham, who was then in charge of the office, told me that Whistler's father had been a star graduate of West Point and a distinguished engineer, and requested me to be attentive to the new appointee ; it may also be for the reason that there was something peculiar about Whistler's person and actions quite at variance with the ordinary run of my experience.

" His style of dress indicated an indifference to fashion which, under circumstances, might be changed into emancipation when fashion, for instance, went into extremes and exacted personal discomforts. I certainly cannot remember Whistler with a high-standing collar and silk hat, which was then the universal custom. Classical models seemed to be his preference, a short circular cloak and broad-brimmed felt hat gave him a finish which reminded one of some of

---

[1] Mr. A. Lindenkohl, now the oldest draughtsman in the department.

Rembrandt's celebrated portraits.   His *tout ensemble* had a
strong tinge of Bohemianism which suggested that his tastes
and habits had been acquired in Paris, or, more concisely
speaking, in the Quartier Latin ; indeed, he always spoke of
Paris with enthusiasm.   His manners were those of an easy
self-reliance which conveyed the impression that he was a
man who minded his own business, but that it would not be
exactly safe to cross his paths.

"At the time of his engagement as draughtsman at the
office not the slightest doubt was entertained of his skill and
ability to fill his post, and it was the principal concern of
Captain Benham to get him sufficiently interested in his
work to engage his serious attention.   It was, however, soon
apparent that he considered topographical drawing as a
tiresome drudgery, and when he was put on etching views
on copper plate, this occupation, although more congenial to
his tastes, was yet too monotonous and mechanical and did
not afford sufficient scope to his peculiar talent for sketching
off-hand figures and to make him feel contented.   Any odd
moment he could snatch from his work he was busy in
throwing off his impromptu compositions on the margins of
his drawings or plate ; odd characters, such as monks, knights,
beggars, seemed to be his favorites.   He was equally skilful
with pen and ink, pencil, brush and sepia after the Spanish
style, or dry point in the English, and often I was struck by
the facility and rapidity with which he evolved his inventions,
there never was the shadow of a dilemma or even hesitancy.

"From the very start he never was punctual in attendance,
and as time wore on he would absent himself for days and
weeks without tendering any excuse.   As far as I remember,
nobody, except Captain Benham, cared to speak to Whistler
about his irregularity, for the reason that it was certain that
no thanks would be earned and that it would not have made
the slightest difference in his habits.   Howsoever that may
have been, Colonel Porterfield, the clerk, was a strict ac-
countant, and his monthly reports told the whole story.

Thus in one month two days were deducted from Whistler's pay for time lost in coming late to office, and in January, 1855, he was credited with but six and one-half days' work, which reduced his scant pay to a mere pittance.

"Under these circumstances three months were quite sufficient length of time for Whistler and the office to realize that the employment of Whistler as a draughtsman was an experiment destined to be a failure, and I do not think that a trace of ill feeling was retained when it was concluded by both parties to effect a separation and let each one go his own way."

At that time Edward de Stoeckl was charge d'affaires of the Russian embassy. He had known Major Whistler in St. Petersburg, and he took a great fancy to his son.

One day Whistler invited him to dinner, and this is the account of what happened :

"Whistler engaged a carriage and called for his distinguished friend. As they drove on, Whistler turned to the diplomat and asked him if he would object to their stopping at several places on the way. M. de Stoeckl, amused at the unconventionality of the request, assented, and his young host then directed the coachman to a greengrocer's, a confectioner's, a tobacconist's, and to several other tradesmen.

"After visiting each of these he would reappear with his arms filled with packages, which he deposited on the vacant seat of the carriage. At last the two brought up at Whistler's lodgings. After a climb up many stairs the representative of the Czar of all the Russias found himself in Whistler's attic.

"Quite out of breath, he was obliged to sit down, too exhausted to speak, during which time Whistler flitted hither and thither, snipping a lettuce into shape for the salad, drying the oysters, browning the biscuit, preparing the cheese, and in an incredibly short time setting a sumptuous repast before his astonished guest, who was delighted with the unique hospitality of the host.''

A comrade in office describes Whistler's appearance in those days :

" He was very handsome, graceful, dressed in good taste, with a leaning towards the style of the artist in the selection of his clothing. His hair was a blue-black and worn very long, and the bushy appearance seemed to give one the impression that each separate hair was curled. Always at this time he wore a large slouch hat and a loose coat, generally unbuttoned, and thrown back so that the waistcoat was plainly seen.''

He never changed very much from that description, save that his hair became slightly gray, and one lock directly over the forehead turned completely white very prematurely. To this white lock Whistler took a great fancy, and it is visible in the portraits and drawings he made of himself. His hair was naturally very curly,—an inheritance from his father,—and out of the mass of black curls the white lock would spring with almost uncanny effect.

To the very end he was extremely fastidious in his dress. In the days when threadbare coats were a luxury he wore them spotlessly clean, and carried old and worn garments in such a manner that they appeared as if made for the occasion.

In his studio and while at work he was never mussy or untidy ; he had more than a woman's notion of neatness.

RECOLLECTIONS AND IMPRESSIONS

He was not only very careful of his clothes, but they must be buttoned and adjusted just so before he would make his appearance. On him a frock coat was never stiff and ungraceful, and somehow he managed to dissipate the dreary formality of evening dress. It was always a pleasure to see him enter a room; while on the street he was, in his earlier London days, exceedingly picturesque.

He was very particular concerning his hats. In the latter Paris days he always wore a most carefully-brushed silk hat with flat brim,—the Quartier-Latin type. This, with his monocle—for on the street he wore a monocle—and his long overcoat, made him an exceedingly striking figure.

One day he was in a shop, trying on a hat, when a dissatisfied customer rushed in, and, mistaking him for some one in charge, said :

"I say, this 'at doesn't fit."

Eyeing him critically a moment, Whistler said :

"Neither does your coat."

Whistler was thoroughly imbued with the military spirit ; and if he had not been a great artist he would have made a good officer. He was born to command, and possessed physical courage of a high order.

In stature and physique he was short and very slight,—could not have weighed more than one hundred and thirty pounds ; but he was so perfectly proportioned that one did not notice his size except when in sharp contrast with others. Notwithstanding his inferiority in size and strength, he never in

his life had the slightest hesitation in striking a man
—even at the risk of annihilation—if he deemed the
occasion required it.

A good many years ago the editor of a gossipy
sheet in London, called the *Hawk*, printed some
items of a personal nature which Whistler resented.
Not knowing the editor by sight, Whistler took a
friend to point him out in the foyer of one of the
London theatres. Although the man was a giant
compared with Whistler, the latter, without a
moment's hesitation, went up to him and struck
him across the face with a cane, saying with each
blow, "Hawk, Hawk, Hawk."

The editor afterwards boasted that he immediately knocked Whistler down. Whistler claimed
he slipped and fell ; but, he said :

"What difference does it make whether he knocked me
down or whether I slipped ? The fact is he was publicly
caned, and what happened afterwards could not offset the
publicity and nature of this chastisement. A gentleman
lightly strikes another in the face with a glove ; the bully
thinks the insult is wiped out if he knocks some one down—
the ethics of the prize ring ; but according to the older
notions the gentleman knows that the soft touch of the glove
cannot be effaced by a blow of the fist,—for if it could, superiority in weight would render the cad and the bully immune.
The historical fact is that I publicly drew my cane across his
face ; no one cares anything about his subsequent ragings, or
whether I slipped and fell, or whether he trampled upon me."

Again, when an artist went up to him in the
Hogarth Club in London and called him a liar and
a coward, Whistler promptly slapped his face.

RECOLLECTIONS AND IMPRESSIONS

So far as controversies with opponents were concerned, he was courageous to the point of indifference ; but, as already noted, in crossing busy streets and making his way through the hurly-burly of city life he was as careful, not to say timid, as a woman ; he had many superstitions which influenced his actions.

One afternoon he said to a sitter :

" To-morrow, you know, we won't work."

" Why not ?"

" Well, you see, it's Friday ; and last Friday, you remember, what a bad time we had,—accomplished nothing. An unlucky day anyway. We'll take a holiday to-morrow."

The military spirit clung to him through life, and he was ever in the habit of referring to his experience at West Point as if it were the one entirely satisfactory episode in his career. He called himself a "West-Pointer," and insisted that the Academy was the one institution in the country the superiority of which to everything of its kind in the world was universally admitted.

" Why, you know, West Point *is* America."

Though living in Paris at the time and the sympathy of all France was with Spain, he lost no opportunity for upholding the United States in the war. He could see no flaw in the attitude or the diplomacy of this country, and was especially eloquent over the treatment of Admiral Cervera after his defeat.

On the other hand, such was his ingrained dislike for England that he lost no opportunity for declaiming against her war in South Africa. He delighted in berating the English and in prodding any English sympathizer who happened in his way.

One day a friend from this side, of Irish birth, but who sided with England, was in his studio, and the discussion waxed warm until the visitor said :

"I'll be dashed if I'll talk with you, Whistler. What do you know about the matter? Nothing at all."

After a short silence, Whistler said :

"But, I say, C——, do you remember how the Boers whipped the Dublin Fusileers?"

Whereupon the air became sulphurous.

The friend afterwards remarked :

"There was nothing in the malicious innuendo anyway, for, you know, those regiments are recruited from all quarters, and there may not have been a single Irishman in the Fusileers at the time of the fight."

Whistler held some extraordinary opinions concerning the Dreyfus case, the outcome of his strong military bias.

It did not matter to him whether the accused was guilty or not, the prestige of the army must be maintained, even at the sacrifice of the innocent,—the view which led the military section of France to such violent extremes against Dreyfus,—and Whistler resented the assaults upon the army as treachery to the most sacred institution of the state.

To the civilian this military bias which leads men in all countries to such extremes in judgments and actions is incomprehensible. The attitude of the military mind towards the ordinary problems of life, towards the faults and failings of men, towards petty transgressions and disobediences, towards rank, routine, and discipline, towards the courtesies and sympathies and affections which are the leavening influences of life, cannot be understood by the lay mind. The soldier's training and occupation are such that he does not think, feel, and act as an ordinary man ; his standards, convictions, and ethics are fundamentally different ; so different that he requires his own territory, his own laws, and his own tribunals. With the soldier the maxim of ordinary justice that it is better that ten guilty should go free than one innocent be condemned is reversed.

By birth, by tradition, by association, Whistler was thoroughly saturated with this spirit ; and it affected his conduct and his attitude towards people throughout his life. It accounts for much of the impatience, the arrogance, the intolerance, the combativeness, the indifference to the feelings of others with which he is charged, or rather overcharged, for much of what is said is exaggeration.

No man can be reared in an atmosphere of authority and blind obedience to authority without losing something of that give-and-take spirit which softens life's asperities.

Therefore, in any estimate of Whistler's character and of his conduct towards others, the influence of these very unusual early associations and conditions must be taken into account and due allowance made.

OF JAMES A. McNEILL WHISTLER

III

An American—The Puritan Element—Attitude of England and France—Racial and Universal Qualities in Art—Art-Loving Nations.

OF Whistler's innate and aggressive Americanism this is the place to speak.

English in origin, the family became Irish and then American. In blood he was doubly removed from England, first by Irish progenitors, then by American, and in his entire make-up, physical and intellectual, he was so absolutely un-English that to the day of his death he was an object of curious observation and wondering comment wherever he went, in even so cosmopolitan a city as London.

There was nothing he loved better than to surprise, mystify, confuse, and confound the stolid Briton. And though he lived most of his life in Chelsea and came back there to spend his last days, he was from the very beginning and remained until the end a stranger in a strange land, a solitary soul in the midst of an uncongenial, unsympathetic, unappreciative, unloving people.

So little does England care for him or his art, or, more truly, so prejudiced is the nation against him as an impertinent interloper, who for more than a generation disturbed the serenity of her art household, that the National Museum has no example of his work. Needless to say, if he had been English, or had come from the remotest of England's outlying possessions, English paperdom and English officialdom would have claimed him as their own, condoned his eccentricities, and bought his works with liberal hand.

During the days of his greatest poverty and distress, when even France turned stupidly aside from things she soon came to worship, and England was jeering clumsily, and all nations repudiated him,—our own the loudest of all,—he really seemed to be "a man without a country," and, beyond question, the injustice, the bitterness of it all entered deep into his soul and remained. But whatever the folly, the blindness, the stupidity of a country, though it seek to cast off a child so brilliant he is not understood, the ties remain ; however strained, they cannot be broken. Nothing that America can do suffices to make an Englishman or a Frenchman or a German out of an American,—the man himself may take on a foreign veneer, but beneath the surface he belongs where blood and birth have placed him.

He was infinitely more of an American than thousands who live at home and ape the manners of Europe. He came from a line of ancestors so distinctively and aggressively American that he could not have turned out otherwise had he tried.

OF JAMES A. McNEILL WHISTLER

He was not even an Anglo-American or a Franco-American, but of all the types and races which go to make the American people he was in blood, appearance, alertness, combativeness, wit, and a thousand and one traits, an exceedingly refined illustration of the Irish-American ; and because of his Irish blood, with perhaps some Scotch on his mother's side, he was never in sympathy with anything English, but was now and then somewhat in sympathy with many things French, though the points of sympathetic contact were so slight and superficial that he could not live contentedly for any length of time in Paris.   In his art, his convictions, and his conventions he was altogether too profound, too serious, too earnest—one might with truth say, too puritanical—to find the atmosphere of Paris altogether congenial.   His great portraits might have come from the studio of a Covenanter, but never from a typical Paris atelier.

The Puritan element which is to be found in every American achievement, whether in war, in art, or in literature, though often deeply hidden, is conspicuous in Whistler's work, though he himself would probably have been the first to deny it ; and it is this element of sobriety, of steadfastness, of undeviating adherence to convictions and ideals that constitutes the firm foundation of his art, of his many brilliant and beautiful superstructures of fancy.

Only a Puritan at heart could have painted the

"Carlyle," "His Mother," and that wonderful child portrait, "Miss Alexander."

Only a Puritan at heart could have painted the mystery of night with all his tender, loving, religious sympathy.

Only a Puritan at heart could have exhibited as he did in everything he touched those infinitely precious qualities of reserve, of delicacy, of refinement, which are the conspicuous characteristics of his work.

Concerning his refinement some one has very truly remarked :

> "He so hated everything ugly or unclean that, even in the club smoking-rooms (where one may sometimes hear rather Rabelaisian tales), he never told a story which could not have been repeated in the presence of modest women. His personal daintiness was extreme. Threadbare coats on him were never shabby. He had to wear too many threadbare garments, poor fellow ! for, inasmuch as he put the integrity of his art before everything else, he never stooped to make those 'pretty' things which would have brought him a fortune, without doubt. He was abstemious in his living, simple in all that he did,—his exquisite, sure taste preventing him from extremes, gaudiness, or untidiness."

And when he lent his support, some eight years ago, to the school kept by Carmen Rossi, who as a child had been one of his models, he would not tolerate the study of the nude by mixed classes, and, in fact, introduced many rules and restrictions which were considered by even American pupils as "puritanical" in the extreme, and which the French could not understand at all.

Harmony in Gray and Green.
Portrait of Miss Alexander

OF JAMES A. McNEILL WHISTLER

He never painted any large and aggressive nudes, such as abound in French art, such as, in a way, may be said to characterize French art and mark its attitude towards life ; but he made many drawings in water-color and pastel, and painted some oils, all, however, exquisitely refined, the element of the nude being in every instance subordinated to the artistic scheme and intention. Many of these drawings have never been exhibited. When seen they will go far towards demonstrating the puritanical element in Whistler.

In his intolerance towards the methods, convictions, and ideals of others he exhibited some of the spirit of the Puritan zealot who knows no creed but his own.

Concerning his Americanism, one who knew him says :[1]

"Upon the known facts of Whistler's career I do not touch. I wish only to underline his Americanism, and to offer you one or two personal memories. He was 'an American of the Americans,' say the American papers, and who shall venture to dispute their dictum ? Not I, certainly. Nor would anybody who knew Whistler personally. I knew him for many years in London and in Paris. I have many letters from him on art and other matters, some of which ought to be printed, for his letters to friends were not less works of art than those which he composed more carefully for print. I have books and drawings which he gave me. I mention these things as evidence that I may fairly say something about him, at least on the personal side. And I

---

[1] G. W. Smalley, in the London *Times*.

knew on what terms he lived with the so-called art world in England, and what his own view of the matter was.''

And an English writer said, some ten years ago :[1]

''It should not be forgotten in America that Mr. Whistler is an American of Americans. It may therefore be appropriately asked, What has America done for him? It has treated him with—if possible—even more ignorance than England ; this, of course, coming from the desire of the Anglomaniac to out-English the English.''

And there are others whose testimony will be forthcoming some day to show how wholly and absolutely American he was to the very core and centre of his being, and in his attitude towards all countries and peoples of Europe.

It is true he said many harsh, bitter, and cutting things concerning the press and people of this country, that he frequently exhibited in the English sections of art exhibitions in preference to those of his own country ; but for all these things there were many good reasons, and we have but ourselves to blame.

He was so much of an American that a single word of ridicule from this side cut deeper than pages of abuse from the other. To the scoffings of England he turned a careless ear, and replied with flippant, but pointed, tongue ; while the utter lack of support and appreciation from his own country was ever referred to with a bitterness that betrayed

---

[1] *The Nation*, vol. liv., pp. 280–281, April 14, 1892.

his real feelings.   He could not understand how the American people could desert a countryman battling alone against all England.   As he frequently said :

" It did not matter whether I was in the right or in the wrong,—I was one against the mob.   Why did America take the side of the mob,—and—and get whipped ?"

America was blind to his merits until long after he achieved fame in every country of Europe ; and it is undeniably true that the press here truculently echoed the slurs of the critics on the other side throughout that long period of controversy.   It is a lamentable fact that up to the day of his death he was misunderstood, or accepted as an eccentric in many quarters of the land that now claims him as her bright particular star in the firmament of art. Notwithstanding all these things, he remained so conspicuously an American that every Englishman and every Frenchman with whom he came in contact recognized him as a foreigner ; neither would have thought of mistaking him for a fellow-countryman ; he was as un-English and un-French as an Italian, or a Spaniard, or—better—as an American.

The "White Girl" was rejected at the Salon in 1863 ; the "Portrait of my Mother" was accepted by the Royal Academy and obscurely hung in 1871, only after a bitter discussion, in which the one member of the committee who favored it, Sir William

Boxall, a friend of Whistler's family, threatened to resign unless it was accepted.

This same great portrait—it is said on good authority—was offered in New York for twelve hundred dollars and found no buyer.

When exhibited in London, language failed to express the full measure of the scorn and contempt the English press—from the ponderous *Times* down to the most insignificant fly-sheet—had for this wonderful picture ; but no sooner had the French government purchased it for the Luxembourg than all was changed, and with delightful effrontery the *Illustrated London News* said :

" Modern *British* (!) art will now be represented in the National Gallery of the Luxembourg by one of the finest paintings due to the brush of an *English* (!) artist,—namely, Mr. Whistler's portrait of his mother."

The italics and exclamation marks are Whistler's own, and his denial of British complicity is complete.

Aside from Whistler's personality, his art finds its only congenial place in the midst of American art.

That his pictures will not hang in any conceivable exhibition of British art without the incongruity being painfully perceptible goes without saying, and none knows this better than English painters themselves.

Of all the various manifestations of art with which Whistler's has come in sharp contrast, English painting has been the slowest and most stubborn in yield-

ing to influences from the far East; whereas of all
painters of the nineteenth century Whistler was the
very first to recognize the wondrous qualities of
Chinese and Japanese art and absorb what those
countries had to teach concerning line and color;
and in so far as the painters of England, and more
conspicuously those of Scotland, have learned aught
of the subtleties and refinements of the East, they
have learned it *through Whistler*, and not direct.

In other words, Whistler has been absolutely immune to English influences ; there is not the faintest
trace in any of his works, etchings, lithographs, or
paintings.   In temperament, mood, fancy, and imagination, in what he saw and the manner that he
painted it, he was as far removed from any " English
School" as Hokusai himself.

On the other hand, England for some time has not
been immune to his influence, and things after—a
long way after—Whistler appear at every exhibition.
What is known as the " Glasgow School"—that body
of able and progressive painters—long ago frankly
accepted him as master.

Of English painters dead and living he had a
poor—possibly too poor—opinion.   He frequently
said, " England never produced but one painter,
and that was Hogarth."   In mellower moments he
would say not unkind things of certain qualities in
other men ; towards the living painters who appreciated his art he was oftentimes generous in the be-
stowal of praise.   But it was impossible for Whistler
to say a thing was good if he did not think so ; and

he would exercise all his ingenuity to get out of expressing an opinion when he knew his real opinion would hurt the feelings of a friend. Towards strangers and enemies he was often almost brutal in condemning what was bad,—as when a rich man took him over his new house, dwelling with pride and enthusiasm on this extraordinary feature and that, at each of which Whistler would exclaim, "Amazing, amazing!" until at the end of their tour of the rooms and halls, he at last said, "Amazing,—and there's no excuse for it!"

Of his attitude towards others a friendly writer said :[1]

"He was not a devotee of Turner, but he yielded to no man in appreciation of certain of the works of that painter. He was not lavish of praise where his contemporaries were concerned. Though he could say pleasant things about them in a rather vague way,—calling some young painter 'a good fellow,' and so on,—words of explicit admiration he did not promiscuously bestow. The truth is, there was an immense amount of stuff which he saw in the exhibitions which he frankly detested. Yet conversation with him did not leave the impression that he was a man grudging of praise. It was rather that a picture had to be exceptionally good to excite his emotions. One point is significant. It was not the flashy and popular painter that he invited to share in the gatherings for which his Paris studio was noted : it was the painter like Puvis de Chavannes, the man who had greatness in him."

---

[1] New York *Tribune*, July 26, 1903.

OF JAMES A. McNEILL WHISTLER

That he had nothing in common with English art, the English were quick to assert, until his fame made him a desirable acquisition, when on this side, and that within the last few years, a disposition to claim him—very much as the business-like empire seizes desirable territory here and there about the globe— has begun to show itself; and, unless America is alert, Whistler will yet appear in the National Gallery as —to quote again the words of the *Illustrated News* —"An English artist."

As regards the French, they are disposed to claim Whistler on three grounds :

First. That he was a student there,—with a master who taught him nothing.

Second. That France acknowledged his genius by the purchase of the portrait of his mother,— twenty years after it was painted, and seven after it was exhibited in Paris.

Third. That he lived for a time in Paris.

Three reasons which would annex to France about every American artist of note, for most of them (1) studied in France, (2) are represented in the Luxembourg, and (3) have lived in Paris much longer than Whistler.

As for those first few years in Paris, even the French concede that Gleyre was entirely without influence upon Whistler's subsequent career.

As regards the recognition of his genius, France was exceedingly slow. The portrait of his mother was exhibited in London in 1871, and purchased for the Luxembourg in 1891, though it had been awarded a medal at the Salon some seven years before.

France no more taught Whistler to paint than it taught him to etch. His masters were older and greater than the art of France. Before he was twenty-five he had absorbed all and rejected most that France had to teach. At twenty-eight he painted a picture which, scorned by the Salon, startled all who visited the "Salon des Refusés," and then—still under thirty—he shook the dust of France from his feet, obliterated every vestige of her influence from his art, and started out to make his way alone and unaided in the domain of the beautiful.

In 1865 he again stirred the critics with that novel creation of color "The Princess of the Land of Porcelain." Nothing of the kind had ever been seen in either French or any other art. It was the application of Western methods to Eastern motives ; it was plainly a study primarily in color, secondarily in line, not at all in character. It was the first great step taken by the Western world towards abstract art.

"The Princess of the Land of Porcelain," the "Lange Leizen," the "Gold Screen," the "Balcony"—all early pictures—are all one and the same in motive ; they are his first attempts in a large way to produce color harmonies, to subordinate everything to the color composition.

The Lange Leizen – of the
Six Marks – Purple and Rose

OF JAMES A. McNEILL WHISTLER

Of Whistler and American art in those days an unnamed correspondent has written from Paris :[1]

"It would puzzle the analysis of a competent critic to find what Whistler owed to Gleyre ; and the young American openly professed to have profited by the counter example of Gustave Courbet, who was the realist of that day. From the first triumph of Courbet in 1849, Gleyre had shrunk back into his shell and no longer exhibited at the annual salons.

"From the start Whistler was an independent ; and when, after six years of work in the studios, he offered a picture for the judgment of the official Salon, the jury promptly refused it. Whistler was not discouraged, and hung the painting in the outlaws' Salon des Refusés. It created a stir that was almost enthusiasm, and the name of his 'Fille Blanche'— White Maiden—was still remembered when four years later a few American painters demanded a section for their work at the Universal Exposition of 1867. I have looked up a criticism of the time, and imagine it will be found more interesting now than when it was written.

"'The United States of America are surely a great country and the North Americans a great people, but what little artists they are ! The big daubs which they exhibit, under pretence of "Blue Mountains," "Niagara Falls," "Genesee Plain," or "Rain in the Tropics," show as much childish arrogance as boyish ignorance. People say that these loud placards are sold for crazy prices in Philadelphia or Boston. I am willing to believe it, but I cannot rejoice at it.'

"This is laid on with no light brush, and some of us can recall the American painters of that remote age who were so mishandled. But the remaining paragraph of the lines given to American art may surprise those who look on Whistler as only a contemporary.

---

[1] New York *Evening Post*, August 1, 1903.

RECOLLECTIONS AND IMPRESSIONS

" 'M. Whistler seems to me the only American artist really worthy of attention ; he is our old acquaintance of the Salon des Refuses of 1863, where his "Fille Blanche" had a *suces d'engouement* (a success of infatuation !).   He is truly an American, as understood by the motto, "time is money." M. Whistler so well knows the value of time that he scarcely stops at the small points of execution ; the impression seized as it flies and fixed as soon as possible in swift strokes, with a galloping brush—such is the artist and such, too, is the man.'

"Velasquez was already in the air, but Japanese art, to which Whistler afterwards allowed himself to be thought indebted, was not yet spoken of.   Thus the young American artist was the precursor of movements which years afterwards came to a head, and which for the most part he has outlived.   In view of this, the closing verdict of the official critic of 1867 is worth noting, the more so as it shows the reward already attributed to the American's industry in another branch of art.   'While waiting for M. Whistler to become a painter in the sense which old Europe still attaches to the word, he is already an etcher (*aquafortiste*), all fire and color, and very worthy of attention, even if he had only this claim to it.' "

Before France cared very much for Velasquez, before it so much as knew there was an island called Japan on the art map, Whistler was playing with the blacks and grays of the master of Madrid and with the blues and silvery whites of the porcelains of the Orient.

And it was he,—Whistler,—the American, who turned the face of France towards the East, and made her see things in line and color her most vagrant fancy had never before conceived.

Searching the shops of Amsterdam, he found the

blue-and-white china which gave him inspiration to do those things beside which the finest art of France is crude and barbaric.

Not very long ago a French writer said, "There is not, as yet, an American school of painting, but there are already many American painters, and great ones, who will in time form a school."

Let us hope not.

A friend—a painter—once called Whistler's attention to several very good things by Alfred Stevens. Whistler looked at them a moment, then said, "School, school, school," and turned away.

In that, or any other restrictive or regulative sense of the word, let us hope there will be no "American school;" but so long as there are American painters there will be American paintings ; and the greater the work the more completely will it reflect the man, and the greater the man the more surely and subtly will it reflect his nationality.

The phrase "American painters" means something more than Americans who paint, and "American paintings" implies the transmission to the work of something of the painter's individuality, which includes as an important element his racial and national characteristics.

In other words, American painters, regardless of where they are trained, where they work, and what they paint, must produce American paintings ; they cannot wholly eliminate their individuality and nationality ; they cannot become so completely French

or English as to absolutely obliterate every trace of
their American origin, and their works, though English, French, or Italian to the last degree, will still
exhibit traces of American origin.   So true is this,
that the paintings of men who have lived longest
abroad and tried hardest to paint after the manner
of others find their most congenial surroundings
amidst American art.

So long as we have American paintings we shall
have an American "school" in the sense that all
American paintings taken together, whether few or
many, whether good or bad, will be distinguished
and distinguishable from the paintings of every other
country.   In that sense America has, and always has
had, a "school" of painting, though for a long time
the school was little more than a kindergarten.

America has no centre like Paris, or Rome, or
Florence, where a large body of men and women
are gathered from the four quarters of the globe to
study art.   In that sense America has no "school;"
but that sort of a "school" is about the worst thing
that can happen to a country.   These great centres
for the diffusion of art are usually fatal to the development of native art ; the presence of a horde of
foreigners, each with his own peculiarities and characteristics, some with the effeminacy of the South,
others with the brutal force and overpowering virilty
of the North, stifles national initiative and produces
sterile cosmopolites.

Paris, with its salons, exhibitions, competitions,

medals, prizes, and innumerable incentives towards commercial, blatant, and vicious art, is the curse of French art, and pretty soon France will have no art that is really hers.

The atmosphere of Paris is one of strenuous striving after effect, of mighty endeavor to make an impression; it encourages facility, dash, bravura, eccentricities, and experiments of all kinds. From the depths of our hearts let us be thankful that America has no "school" of that kind, and earnestly hope that American artists residing temporarily within that atmosphere will be affected as little as was Whistler.

Paris is an æsthetic Babel.

The art of Greece was suffocated when the entire coast-line of the Mediterranean came to study the Acropolis.

Turning to the entire body of American painters, at home and abroad, we find that they constitute at the present day the one "school" that has already given to the world the greatest artist since the days of Rembrandt and Velasquez,—and greater than either in some respects, as we shall see,—and also the greatest of living portrait-painters, not to mention a half-dozen more who are recognized internationally as masters in their chosen fields; the one "school" that contains more of sobriety, more of sanity, more of youthful vigor and virility, more of indomitable energy and perseverance, more of promise and assurance of mighty achievement than

all the schools of all the other nations taken together.

If the world is destined to see the modern equiv-
alent of ancient Athens, it will be somewhere within
the confines of North America.

The countries of the Old World have had their
opportunities, and the tide of progress in its circuit
of the globe is already lapping the shores of the
Western continent.

In temperament the typical American lies about
midway between the stolidity of the Englishman
and the volatility of the Frenchman. He has much
of the dogged perseverance of the former, with a
large element of the facility and versatility of the
latter; he is steadfast in the pursuit of his ideals,
and at the same time quick to adopt new and improved methods for attaining his ends; he has an
Englishman's tenacity of conviction and much of a
Frenchman's brilliancy of expression. As compared
with an Englishman the American appears more
than half French; as compared with a Frenchman he seems essentially English. It is this combination of earnest convictions, profound belief in
self and country, sobriety, perseverance, tenacity of
purpose, stolid endurance, with inventiveness, originality, irresistible impulsiveness, dash and brilliancy
in execution, that assures to the future of North
America the noblest of human achievements.

For the present the strength and resources of the
country are absorbed in the production of wealth;
but soon the people will tire of this pursuit, and the

OF JAMES A. McNEILL WHISTLER

accumulated wealth of nation, States, cities, and individuals will turn to the encouragement of things
beautiful in not only art and literature, but in the
long-neglected handicrafts,—the crafts that make
instead of destroying men.

At the World's Exposition of 1893, in Chicago,
Whistler's paintings hung, where they rightfully be-
longed, in the American section.   Though far and
away superior to anything in the entire section, and
conspicuous above everything near for their exquisite
beauty, still it cannot be gainsaid that of all the sections of that exhibition the American was the only
one which would contain Whistler's work without
the contrast being so marked as to be absolutely
destructive.   That they could not hang with entire
fitness among the English pictures even the English
would admit ; that their sober harmonies were distinctively at variance with the brilliant and superficial qualities of the French pictures was apparent
to even the unpractised eye.   "The Yellow Buskin"
and "The Fur Jacket," to mention no others, could
hang in only one place, and that was where they
were put,—in the main hall of the American section,
flanked and confronted by American work.

Not that the pictures about them equalled in
merit,—that is not the question ; but they were sufficiently akin to constitute an harmonious environment.

Art is simply a mode of expression, and the
highest, truest, noblest art is the reflection of the

5   65

best there is in a people. It follows, therefore, that the art of any race or people must exhibit the racial characteristics. A painting, for instance, belongs first to the man who painted it and bears on its face so many marks of his individuality that not only he but others recognize it as his. Secondly, the painting belongs to the race or people with which the artist is identified, for the very traits which distinguish him as an American, or an Englishman, or a Frenchman from all other nationalities inevitably make themselves felt in the work, and distinguish it not only specifically from all other canvases, but generically from the work of other peoples, schools, epochs, eras, etc.

A man may change his allegiance and live in foreign lands, but he cannot change his blood. If a Chinaman, he will remain a Chinaman, no matter where he lives ; if an American, he will remain an American, though, like many of our mess-of-pottage citizens, he may remain a bastard American in the endeavor to become an adopted Englishman.

The finer the art the more universal its qualities. And yet there is no poem and no picture that is absolutely without the marks of its master ; and the marks of the master mean the marks of his race,— in fact, the racial indications are inversely in number to those of the individual ; the deeper a man buries his personality in his work the stronger the indications of his race. Shakespeare so lost himself that his personal characteristics nowhere appear in his great plays, and a conception of the poet's personality could not be formed from a reading of the lines—so universal was his genius; yet his poetry is essentially and everlastingly English,—far more conspicuously English than the poetry of lesser men who sing about England and things English. It is more English than Chaucer, more English than Spencer, more English than Browning, Tennyson, or Swinburne; it breathes more fully and more truly the spirit of the English people in their greatest days than any poetry ever uttered by the English tongue.

The greater the man, the more completely does he express his people. It takes a great race to produce a great man; and once produced, he is everlastingly linked with his tribe.

But greatness implies the suppression of the petty, including all petty resemblances; therefore, a man by the universal qualities of his genius may seem to belong to the world, whereas in truth he is but the expression of the best there is in his countrymen.

Rembrandt suppressed all provincialisms and seemed to etch and paint for mankind rather than for a limited public in Holland; and yet to the last he was simply the greatest of Dutch artists. And because he was so essentially and truly Dutch he is one of the world's great artists; in the chorus of the world's proud voices there is no mistaking his accent.

RECOLLECTIONS AND IMPRESSIONS

Velasquez is at the same time the least Spanish of painters and the most Spanish of artists. Suppressing all eccentricities of time and place, he rose to universal heights, and the world claims him as its own; and yet his fame depends upon the fact that he was from first to last a Spaniard,—a Spaniard in precisely the sense that Cervantes was the expression of inarticulate forces behind him. Deriving more or less help from his contemporaries, and from this quarter and that, from the visit of Rubens and from his own journey to Italy, he, after all, was the achievement of the Spanish people in painting. He was not an Italian, he was not a Frenchman, he was not a Dutchman,—he was a Spaniard of the Spaniards, as Shakespeare was an Englishman of the English.

Having wandered far afield in the endeavor to point out the intimate connection between, first, a man and his work,—which connection every one admits,—and, secondly, between the race and the work,—a connection which is not so readily perceived,—let us return to Whistler, whose work furnishes proof positive of what has been said.

It is commonly taken for granted that if a man lives and studies and works abroad for many years he loses his individuality and becomes in some mysterous manner the offspring of the country where he works. It is assumed that American painters residing in Rome become more or less Italian; that those residing in Paris become more or less French;

that those residing in London become more or less English ; while those who move restlessly from place to place become more or less of characterless cosmopolites. All of which is true inversely to the real strength and genius of the artist. A weak man is swerved by this influence and that and—chameleon like—takes on the hues of his surroundings, but a strong man simply absorbs and assimilates without in the slightest degree losing his individuality. Unhappily, many American artists residing abroad possess so little stamina, so little of real character, so little of genius, that they are—like topers—dependent upon the daily stimulus afforded by the manifold art activities about them ; they never get out of school, but remain helplessly dependent upon teachers and copy-books. The annual Salon, like a college commencement day, is their great incentive ; their petty exhibitions are so many field-days necessary to sustain childish enthusiasm.

Happily, all do not yield to those influences, and no two yield in precisely the same degree,—the extent to which individuality is lost depending upon the weakness of the man. A poor, weak, wishy-washy American quickly falls into the habit of painting pictures after the manner of those about him, and his mannerisms out-Herod Herod ; others, with more character, yield less to their environment ; while the chosen few simply absorb whatever of good they find, and without yielding a jot of their individuality, without swerving to the right or to the left, go on producing after their own fashion things which belong to them and the race that produced them.

For more than forty years Whistler was the conspicuous example of the last-named class,—a class so small that it included besides himself—no others.

Great as certain of our American artists residing abroad undoubtedly are, good as many of these surely are, creditable on the whole as all are to American art, there is not one whose work does not betray the influences of his environment; there is not one who has not sacrificed something of his originality, something of his strength, something of his native force and character on strange altars, saving and excepting, always, Whistler.

The most that men have ventured to say is that he was influenced by Velasquez, though he himself has said he never visited Madrid,—a statement many insist cannot be true; others say he has been influenced by Japanese art,—but Velasquez and the art of Japan are far from French or English art of the nineteenth century; and the assertion that he was influenced by either is a confession that he lived unscathed amidst his surroundings.

Back of the art of Japan is the purer art of China; and to that source must we go if we seek the factors that influenced Whistler, for he loved the porcelain and pottery of China long before they were collected by the museums and amateurs of Europe.

"When no one cared for it," he said, "I used to find in Amsterdam the most beautiful blue-and-white china. That was a good many years ago ; it is all gone now."

Old Delft did not inspire him with any enthusiasm. "Crude, crude, crude."

This art of China, as reflected and elaborated in that of Japan, influenced him,—of that there can be no doubt,—and he recognized what was good in Japanese art before others gave it any attention.

The art of Velasquez had its due weight, for he loved the work of the Spanish master ; and if he never visited Madrid, perhaps it was because he feared falling too much under its influence. But he went frequently to the Louvre, and invariably to the little "Infanta," which he would look at long and earnestly, and to Titian's "Man with the Glove," which was a favorite, and to certain Rembrandts, and to Franz Hals, and a few, a very few others,— the gems of the collection,—ignoring completely the pictures which commonly attract, never once glancing up at the huge canvases by Rubens and his pupils ; in fact, so far as he was concerned the walls might have been bare save for a half-dozen masterpieces ; and these he really did love. There was no mistaking his attitude towards them. It was one of reverential affection. He appreciated a really good thing, whether he or some one else had done it, and he hated above everything sham and pretence and foolish display. To him a picture the size of one's hand, if well and conscientiously done, was just as important as a full-length portrait.

The Italian masters influenced him, for he often

spoke of them, of the wonderful effects they obtained with such simple materials and such straightforward methods ; their mastery of color influenced him, and he sought, so far as possible, to discover the pigments and the methods they used.

Those are the factors which helped to make Whistler,—the purest art ; he was not influenced by what went on about him, or by what was said about him. So little did he care what others were doing or how they did it that his very brushes and pigments were different ; and his methods were so peculiarly his own that no one painted at all like him, and his fellow-artists looked on in amazement.

The wave of impressionism which submerged all Paris in the very midst of his career left him unaffected,—for his art was an older and truer impressionism, an impressionism that did not depend upon the size of brushes or the consistency of pigments.

A visitor once said to him :

" Mr. Whistler, it seems to me you do not use some of those very expensive and brilliant colors which are in vogue nowadays."

" No." And he diligently worked away at his palette. " I can't afford to,—they are so apt to spoil the picture."

" But they are effective."

" For how long ? A year, or a score of years, perhaps ; but who can tell what they will be a century or five centuries hence. The old masters used simple pigments which they ground themselves. I try

OF JAMES A. McNEILL WHISTLER

to use what they used. After all, it is not so much
what one uses as the way it is used."

Much of the foregoing argument concerning the
Americanism of Whistler and his art may seem to
be contradicted by his own express utterances.

For did he not say in his "Ten o'Clock"?

"Listen! There never was an artistic period."

"There never was an art-loving nation."

And he pointed out how the man who, "differing
from the rest," who "stayed by the tents with the
women and traced strange devices with a burnt stick
upon a gourd, . . . who took no joy in the ways of
his brethren, . . . who perceived in nature about
him curious curvings, as faces are seen in the fire,
this dreamer apart, was the first artist."

"And presently there came to this man another—
and, in time, others—of like nature, chosen by the
gods ; and so they worked together ; and soon they
fashioned, from the moistened earth, forms re-
sembling the gourd. And with the power of creation, the heirloom of the artist, presently they went
beyond the slovenly suggestion of nature, and the
first vase was born, in beautiful proportion."

And the toilers and the heroes were athrist, "and
all drank alike from the artist's goblets, fashioned
cunningly, taking no note the while of the crafts-
man's pride, and understanding not his glory in his
work ; drinking at the cup, not from choice, not from
a consciousness that it was beautiful, but because,
forsooth, there was no other !"

73

RECOLLECTIONS AND IMPRESSIONS

"And the people questioned not, *and had nothing to say in the matter.*"

"So Greece was in its splendor, and art reigned supreme,—by force of fact, not by election,—and there was no meddling by the outsider."

Again he says :

"The master stands in no relation to the moment at which he occurs a monument of isolation, hinting at sadness, having no part in the progress of his fellow-men."

Those are the propositions which called out the reply—positive and intemperate—from Swinburne,[1] and so estranged the two, and which to this day have proved huge stumbling-blocks in the paths of those who try to understand Whistler.

For the world does believe that there have been "artistic periods," that there have been "art-loving nations," that in some mysterious manner the master does stand in "relation to the moment at which he occurs."

And the world is right ; though it does not necessarily follow that Whistler was wrong in the particular views he had in mind when he uttered his epigrammatic propositions.

In one sense it is undoubtedly true that the master does seem to stand apart, "a mouument of isolation," that he does seem to happen without any causal connection with either parents or country,

---

[1] *Fortnightly Review*, June, 1888.

time or place,—for who could have fortold the greatness of Shakespeare from an acquaintance with those
obscure individuals his father and mother, or from
a knowledge of Stratford and its environs?   Who
could have predicted the triumphs of Napoleon
from a study of his Corsican forbears, or the strange
genius of Lincoln from his illiterate progenitors and
humble surroundings, or the elemental force of
Walt Whitman from his ancestry and American conditions?

No one ; and yet there is the profound conviction
that each of these men, like every great man,—
prophet, king, statesman warrior, poet, or painter,—
appeared, not miraculously, but as the inevitable
result of irresistible forces ; that the brilliant man
is, after all, the son of his parents and the child of
his times.

In the mystery of generation two stupidities fused
in the alembic of maternity produce a genius.

The occasion does not create, but calls forth its
master.   Every war has its great general, every crisis
its great leader, and in the world of art great artists
respond to meet the requirements of the hour.

The bent of a nation determines the occupations
of her sons,—towards war and conquest, towards
peace and industry, towards things artistic or things
commercial, all as the case may be.

It is not the birth of the poet that turns the nation
from commerce to poetry ; it is rather the imperceptible development of the nation itself in the direc-

tion of the ideal that calls into activity—not being—the poet.

Neither race nor nation can by its fiat create a poet; but it can by its encouragement stimulate his activity and rouse him to his best. It could not create a Keats; but it might have urged him on to even greater heights than he attained,—for who can doubt that his clear, pure crystalline song was stifled for lack of appreciation?

Now and then a genius, such as Carlyle, such as Whistler, such as Whitman, asserts himself in spite of all rebuffs, for each of these men pursued his chosen path regardless of all revilings; but, so susceptible is genius to encouragement and discouragement, that, for the most part, it droops before the withering blast of adverse criticism, and only those of hearts so strong and wills so stubborn that opposition inflames them to greater efforts make headway against the world.

It was no one genius that made the monuments and literature of Greece, the art of China and Japan, the paintings of Italy, the Gothic cathedrals of France and England; it was the demand for all these things and their appreciation by those who could not do them that called forth and encouraged the doers.

The first artist may neglect the chase and the field and remain by the tents idly tracing strange designs upon gourds; but unless those who till the soil and bring in the food see his decorated gourds and like them, and prefer them to the plain ones which abound, and are willing to give him food and shelter for his work, he will not remain by the tents very long, and his artistic career will be foreshortened by necessity.

But if the toilers and the hunters like the decorated gourds, and the demand for them increases, others of the tribe who have talent for designing and decoration will join the master and imitate his work, and every now and then a pupil will prove a genius and surpass the "first artist," and art will grow and art-products will multiply, but only so long as the rest of the tribe are willing to work and toil and to exchange the necessaries of life for paintings and carvings and pottery ; and the greater the demand, the keener the desire of the people for decorated things in preference to those that are plain and cheap, the larger will be the chance of uncovering now and then a genius, until, as with the Greeks, the effective demand for things beautiful, for poetry, music, painting, sculpture, and architecture, becomes so great that we have an artistic people and an art-epoch,—that is to say, a people that is only too glad to encourage and support a large number of artists of every kind, and an era when of a given population an unusually large percentage is devoted to the service of the beautiful.

The master does *seem*—as Whistler says—to come unbidden ; but he will not remain long, and others will not follow in his footsteps, unless he arouses at least sufficient appreciation to give him life.

The future of art—of literature, of the drama, and of all the handicrafts—in America depends not upon the coming of a genius, but upon the growth of an effective and irresistible demand for good things ; when that demand is sufficiently imperative, a Phidias, an Angelo, a Shakespeare will respond, for genius is latent everywhere.

The sudden degradation of the arts in Japan within the memory of man was not due to the disappearance of the talent and genius which for nearly a thousand years had been steadily—almost methodically—producing things beautiful, but it was due to the suppression of the feudal system, of those great lords who from the beginning had been the sure patrons of art and supporters of artists, and to the throwing open of ports to the commerce of the world and the introduction of the commercial spirit.

The genius for the creation of beautiful things remains,—for a people does not change in the twinkling of an eye,—but the talent is no longer in demand, or, in many cases, is diverted to the more profitable pursuits of the hour.

IV

Early Days in Paris and Venice—Etchings, Litho-graphs, and Water-Colors—" Propositions" and " Ten o' Clock."

AFTER leaving the coast survey, Whistler went to England, and thence to Paris in 1855, and entered the studio of Charles Gabriel Gleyre, where he remained two years.

Beyond the fact that Whistler was for a time in his studio, Gleyre has not much claim on fame. There could not have been anything in common between the master and his pupil, for he was academic to the last degree. " Not even by a tour in the East did he allow himself to be led away from the classic manner ; and as the head of a great leading studio he recognized it as the task of his life to hand the traditions of the school of Ingres," whom Whistler used to call a " Bourgeois Greek," " on to the present." He " was a man of sound culture, who during a sojourn in Italy, which lasted five years, had examined Etruscan vases and Greek statues with unintermittent zeal, studied the Italian classics, and copied all Raphael. Having come back to Paris, he never drew a line without having first assured himself how Raphael would have proceeded."

However, there must have been a certain combative streak in his character which did appeal to Whistler, for in 1849 he quarreled with the Salon over the success of Courbet, and thereafter sent his pictures to Swiss exhibitions.

Whistler's first commission grew out of an acquaintance made at West Point. At one of the commencement festivities he met a charming young girl, a Miss Sally Williams, and her father, Captain Williams.

While a student in Paris, the pretty daughter and the bluff old captain called on him, and the captain said :

" Mr. Whistler, we are over here to see Paris, and I want you to show us the pictures."

Nothing loath, Whistler took them to the Louvre, and after they had walked a mile or two the captain stopped before some pictures that pleased him and asked :

" Do you suppose you could copy these pictures?"

" Possibly."

" Then, I wish you would copy this, and that, and that," pointing out three paintings. " When they are finished, deliver them to my agent, and he will pay you your price."

Whistler made the copies, and received the first money he ever earned with his brush.

One of these canvases, a copy of an Ingres, turned up in New York a year or two ago. It bore Whistler's signature, but was so atrocious—imagine a combination of Ingres and Whistler—that even

the dealer doubted its authenticity; but when a
photograph was shown Whistler, he recognized the
picture and told the story.

Of these early days many stories are told, but
they are all more or less apocryphal. It is as natural for stories to cluster about Whistler as for bar-
nacles to cling to a ship. He told so many good ones
that, as with Lincoln, innumerable good, bad, and
indifferent which he did not tell are attributed to
him, and thousands are told about him which have
slight foundations in fact.

It is well nigh impossible to sift the true from the
false,—a thing Whistler himself did not attempt,—
though it is possible to sift the wheat from the chaff,
the inane, insipid, and pointless from the bright and
crisp.

Any man can vouch for a story, but who can
vouch for a good story? The story-teller? Heaven
forbid! By all the rules of evidence the testimony
of so interested a witness is inadmissible. The better the story, the more doubtful its authenticity,—
its formal, its literal authenticity. The better the
teller, the more daring his liberties with prosaic details. A good story-teller is a lapidary who receives
his material in the rough and polishes it into a jewel
by removing three-fourths of its substance; or, under
pressure of necessity, he deftly manufactures paste.
To be without stories is the story-teller's crime; a
wit without witticisms is no wit at all, hence the
strain upon veracity.

RECOLLECTIONS AND IMPRESSIONS

Happily, the world conspires to help both wit and story-teller by supplying during their lives, and in great abundance after their deaths, stories and witticisms without end. Give a man the reputation of being a humorist, and all he has to do is to sit discreetly silent and watch his reputation grow. If he really deserves his reputation, he may add to his fame by fresh activities ; but if he is something of a sham, as most wits are, he would better leave his sayings to the imaginations of others.

Whistler's sense of humor was so keen, his wit so sharp, his facility in epigram and clever sayings so extraordinary, that what are genuinely his are better than anything others have said about him ; therefore, it is a pity some one has not jotted down first hand some of the good things that constantly fell from his lips. Perhaps some one has, and his life and sayings will yet appear with all the marks of authority and authenticity.

But his sharp and exceedingly terse sayings often suffer greatly in the telling, frequently to the loss of all point and character. The following instance is in point :

A group of society women were once discussing the graces and accomplishments of Frederic Leighton.

"So handsome."

"Plays divinely."

"Perfectly charming."

"Sings."

82

OF JAMES A. McNEILL WHISTLER

" And is so great a sculptor."

Whereupon Whistler, who was of the party, tim-idly advanced the query :

" Paints a little, too, does he not?"

That is one version of an old and well-worn Whist-ler anecdote, and other versions, which are at all characteristic, do not vary in more than two or three words.

See what the story becomes in the mouth of the incompetent.[1]

" One evening a dozen of us were sitting in Broughton's reception-room, waiting for our carriages to be announced, and Whistler was sitting by himself on a lounge on the other side of the room. We were discussing the versatile talents of Frederic Leighton, one of the leading painters of England, and afterwards president of the Royal Academy. One spoke of his astonishing linguistic accomplishments : he could ex-press himself in every European tongue and in several Ori-ental ones. Another mentioned his distinguished merit as an architect : he was building an addition to his studio which was like a vision of Aladdin or Haroun Al Rashid. Another called attention to his ability in sculpture : a group of an athlete and a serpent was then exhibiting in the Academy, which challenged the works of antique art. Another men-tioned his talent as an orator : no man in London could make a better after-dinner speech. Another praised his per-sonal beauty and grace and his athletic prowess. At length there fell a silence, because all of us had contributed his or her mite of eulogy,—all of us, that is, with the exception of Whistler, reclining on his elbow at the other side of the room.

" By a common impulse we all glanced over at him : what

---

[1] *The Independent*, November 2, 1899.

would he say? He partly raised himself from his lolling attitude and reached for his crush hat on the sofa. 'Yes,' he added, slowly and judicially, as if benevolently confirming all the praise we had poured forth; and then, as if by an after-thought, calling our attention to a singular fact not generally known, 'Yes, and he can paint, too!'"

After all the verbosity, padding, and penny-a-lining, the point is missed by attributing to Whistler the positive averment that Leighton could paint.

Small wonder that the writer in the next paragraph confesses:

"My own crude first attempts to understand Whistler's paintings were dismal failures; and of course I imagined that the failure was in the painting, and not in myself. I could see no beauty in them: the drawing was indeterminate; the colors were not pretty; the pictures all seemed unfinished."

It is less difficult than one would suppose to recall things said by Whistler, for he would repeat a good thing and was always polishing.

For instance, in his controversy with the critics he originally said that "Ruskin's high-sounding, empty things . . . flow of language that would, could he hear it, give Titian the same shock of surprise that was Balaam's when the first great critic proffered his opinion."

A very literal correspondent wrote to the papers that the "ass was right," and quoted the Bible in proof.

Nothing daunted, Whistler acknowledged the hit, saying, "But, I fancy, you will admit that this is the only ass on record who ever did see the Angel of the Lord, and that we are past the age of miracles."

Years after, in referring to the matter, he improved his reply to, "But I fancy you will admit that this is the only ass on record that ever was right, and the age of miracles is past."

His love of epigram was so great that nothing which was terse or pointed escaped his ears or fled his memory.

One day, while lunching with a friend who knew something about the habits and eccentricities of good wine, Whistler was telling about the peculiarities of Henry James, how James would drag a slender incident through several pages until it was exhausted, whereupon his friend casually remarked:

"The best of wine is spoiled by too small a spiggot."

Immediately alert, Whistler said:

"What's that? what's that you said? Did you get that out of Shakespeare?"

"Not at all; it is simply a physical fact that if you let good wine dribble through a small spiggot you lose its fragrance and character."

"God bless me, but I believe you are right; and it's a good saying,—it's James to a—drop."

No doubt there are many still living who knew Whistler in those early Paris days, but if so, few have so far made known their reminiscences. One fellow-student describes one of the places where they used to dine inexpensively as follows :[1]

" In Paris, in the fifties, there existed in the Rue de la Michaudiere what appeared to be an ordinary Paris creamery. In the front shop were sold milk, butter, and eggs. Over the door was the usual painted tin coffee-pot, indicating that *caffé au lait*, and eggs, butter, and rolls could be obtained in the back room.

" The place was kept by Madame Busque, who had been a governess in a private family in the south of France, and having saved a little money, had come to Paris and opened a creamery. The very day she opened her shop, Mr. Chase, Paris correspondent of the New York *Times*, passing by, was attracted by the clean look of the place, and stepped in for his early breakfast of coffee and rolls.[2] The little back room contained two round tables, and beyond was the kitchen with the usual charcoal broiler and little furnaces. Chase was so pleased that he came again, and getting acquainted with Madame, who was well educated and very ladylike and anxious to please, arranged for a dinner at 6.30 for a party of four. Everything was good and so well served that soon she had a regular custom of American residents,—literary men, artists, and students of all kinds, art, scientific, literary, and medical,—and soon the place became famous. American dishes were introduced,—mince and pumpkin pies and buckwheat cakes. It was not easy to reproduce these things in Paris. The pumpkin pie was a trouble. Madame was told how to make it by a man who only knew how it looked and tasted, and who neglected to mention the crust ; and as Madame had no knowledge of pies in general, she served the first pumpkin pie as a soup in a tureen. Just at that time came in a bright young woman, introduced by one of the

---

[1] W. L. B. Jenney, in the *Amer. Architect*, January 1, 1898.

[2] A correspondent writes that it was W. D. Huntingdon of the *Tribune*.

habitués, who offered to come next forenoon and show
Madame Busque how to make a genuine Yankee pumpkin
pie, which she did ; and the pies produced in that little
creamery were famous and were sent out to Americans all
over Paris. Fine carriages, including that of the American
minister, to the amazement of the neighborhood, would call
for these pies to take home.

"Among the *habitués* was young Whistler, then an art
student. He was bright, original, and amusing, but gave at
that time no promise of any particular ability as an artist.
His drawing was careless. I remember one of his pictures,
—a woman seated at the piano, a little child playing on
the floor. The piano was so out of drawing that it looked
as if it were falling over. As students are always fond of
guying each other, one said to Whistler, ' Hurry and put a
fifth leg under that piano or it will fall and smash the baby.'

"One day, in the Luxembourg, Whistler had his easel in a
crowd with others. They were all at work making copies
from a famous picture that had just been added to the gallery. Whistler would paint a bit, and then rush back to
contemplate what he had done. In one of these mad backward rushes he struck a step-ladder on the top of which was
a painter. Over went step-ladder, painter, and all, and the
painter, trying to save himself, seized the top of his own
canvas and another, pulling them over, easels and all. One
knocked down another, and there was a great crash.
Whistler was in the midst, and his loud voice was heard, as
he sat on the floor, his head protruding through a big canvas
that had fallen on him, using expressions of a vigorous type.
He was seized by the guardian, because, as Whistler was
making the most noise, he assumed that the whole fuss was
due to him. This was quite correct ; but all the painters
coming to his rescue, telling the guardian that it was all an
accident, he let Whistler off.

"He organized a company of French negro minstrels,
writing the songs and stories, and gave a performance which

was very amusing. Among the *habitués* at Madame Busque's was a student from the School of Mines, Vinton, afterwards Professor of Mining at Columbia College, and during the war a brigadier-general. He himself told me the following story in 1866. One night in South Carolina an officer wandered into his camp. He sent word to the general by the sergeant of the guard that he was an officer who had lost his way, that he asked permission to pass the rest of the night in his camp, adding that he had known General Vinton when a student in Paris. General Vinton sent for the officer, whom he failed to recognize. After some thought he asked the question, 'Who was the funniest man we knew in Paris?' 'Whistler,' instantly answered the officer. 'All right,' says Vinton; 'take that empty cot; you are no spy.' "

Among the students he knew in those days were Degas, Ribot, and Fantin-Latour, whose work every one knows.

Manet was working up to his best; in 1861 he painted the "Child with a Sword," now in the Metropolitan Museum in New York, and altogether the atmosphere was charged with the strong sulphur of revolution.

In England the pre-Raphaelites—old and new— were turning the hands of time backward, in France the Impressionists were pressing them forward, in both countries the ferment of change was working.

When only twenty-four years of age, in 1858, Whistler's first etchings appeared, published by Delâtre, with a dedication to Seymour Haden, his brother-in-law. In those days the relations between the two men were very cordial; unhappily, not so later, as may be seen in "Gentle Art."

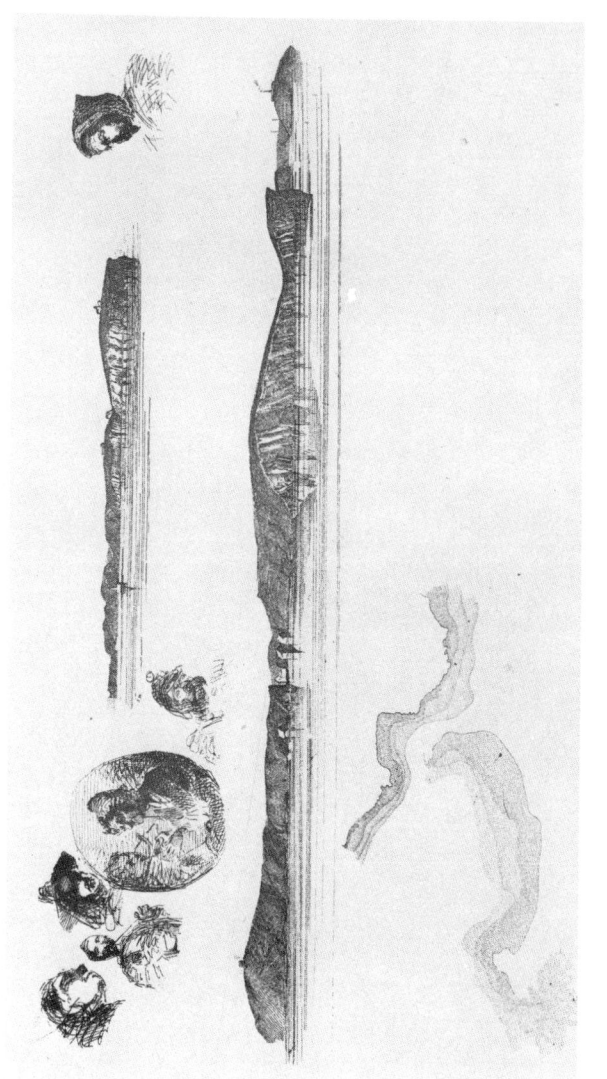

Plate Made While in the Employ of the Government at Washington, 1854-55

OF JAMES A. McNEILL WHISTLER

One of Haden's best plates, "Battersea Beach," bears in its first state this inscription, "Old Chelsea, Seymour Haden, 1863, out of Whistler's window," and another plate of the same year is entitled, "Whistler's House, old Chelsea." [1]

Prior to the publication of the "French Set," Whistler had etched three plates, which are catalogued as [2]

"Early Portrait of Whistler. A young man bare-headed. An impression on which Whistler wrote 'Early Portrait of Self' is in the Avery collection in the Lenox Library, New York.

"Annie Haden. On the only impression known, now in Avery collection, Lenox Library, Whistler wrote, 'Very early ; most probably unique.'

"The Dutchman Holding His Glass. This is signed 'J. W.,' and but two or three impressions are in existence."

There must have been many other early attempts before the "French Set" was formally undertaken, and possibly other plates and prints will come to light in the rigorous search that is sure to be made for everything that he ever did. A plate made while in the service of the coast survey is in existence,—a headland embellished with vagrant heads and figures. Some of the prints are to be seen in collections.

---

[1] Wedmore, Fine Prints, p. 103.
[2] Wedmore's Catalogue, pp. 19–20.

RECOLLECTIONS AND IMPRESSIONS

The "French Set" consisted of twelve plates and an etched title, making thirteen plates in all.

But few copies of the set were printed, and the original price was two guineas per copy.

It is, of course, quite impracticable to give a complete list of Whistler's etchings, for three hundred and seventy-two have been duly listed and described, and it is altogether likely that this number will be increased to over four hundred.

Whistler himself was very careless about keeping either a set of proofs or anything like a memorandum of what he had done. In fact, he did not know what or how many etchings and lithographs he had made or how many pictures he had painted.

Everything he did was so entirely the pleasure of the moment, and each new work, whether large or small, so completely absorbed him, that he quite forgot the labor of yesterday.

All his life long he would begin things and throw them aside, and he would finish things and throw them aside also. To him the only hour of vital import was the present. To the very last his work shows the enthusiasm, the even more than youthful impulsiveness, with which he would begin each new undertaking.

He could never work at an etching, a lithograph, or a painting one moment after it became drudgery; he could never finish a thing simply because he had begun it, or because some one thought it ought to be finished ; hence endless misunderstandings with sitters and patrons, who could not understand why what they had bargained for should not be finished and delivered.

No matter how hard at work on any subject, he was instantly diverted by another which appealed to him more ; and he would leave a sitter who was to pay him a thousand guineas to sketch an Italian urchin.

Unmethodical to the last degree in all his affairs, always absorbed in what he had in hand, it is not surprising that he kept little track of the things he had done.

The first catalogue of his etchings was published in London in 1874. It contained about eighty etchings. In 1886 Mr. Frederick Wedmore catalogued two hundred and fourteen, and in 1899 increased the number to two hundred and sixty-eight.

In 1902 a supplement [1] to Wedmore's catalogue brought the number of known prints up to three hundred and seventy-two.

The "Thames Set," sixteen in number, did not appear publicly as a "set" until 1871, though made many years before ; and the very rare early impressions made by Whistler himself are considered far superior to the prints of 1871 and after.

In 1880 the Fine Arts Society issued the "First Venice Set" of a dozen plates, and in 1886 Messrs. Dowdeswell issued a set of twenty-six, known as the "Twenty-six Etchings."

---

[1] Printed by H. Wunderlich & Co., New York.

RECOLLECTIONS AND IMPRESSIONS

One who knew him in his early Venice days gives the following reminiscences : [1]

"We were often invited to dine with Whistler, whose apartment was on the next flight above. He came to our rooms one day, and said, 'A——, I would like you and B—— to dine with me to-day. You have such a supply of newspapers, please bring several with you, as I have neither papers nor table-cloth, and they will answer the purpose quite well.' I did as he requested, and surprised and amused was our host when I called his attention to a column and a half of 'Whistler stories' in one of the Boston papers, which was serving as our table-cloth.

"One day I called on Whistler when he was engaged in decorating the interior of a house. He lay on his back on the floor, and the handle of the brush was a fish-pole which reached to the ceiling.

"Once a year, in the summer time, it is the custom of Venetians to go to the Lido, a surf-bathing resort, to see the sun rise. They leave in the evening, in gondolas, accompanied with the inevitable mandolin and guitar, and sometimes with an upright piano. The excursionists make a night of it, and Whistler was one of the number. Next day he wished to make a study from our window, the approach to the Grand Canal. Leaving him for a time by himself, upon my return there was a striking study of the view on the easel, and Whistler before the easel asleep. The brushes had fallen from his grasp, and, well charged with fresh paint, were resting in his lap. As he wore white duck trousers, the effect can well be imagined.

"I have often heard him use the word 'pretty,' when looking at a study that had no particular redeeming feature to recommend it. Not wishing to wound the feelings of the artist, he would remark, with that peculiar drawl of his, 'That is pretty, yes, very pretty.'

---

[1] W. S. Adams, in the Springfield *Republican*.

OF JAMES A. McNEILL WHISTLER

"One day he called upon two students. On the wall was the study of a child, most beautifully done by one of them. Whistler stood before it for a long time in deep admiration, and then, turning to the art student, said, ' That is away beyond yourself.' Truly it was, for I called again a few days afterwards, and the body attached to the beautiful head was not worthy the brush of a five-years-old child. And I wondered how such incongruous things could be.

"Whistler was very loyal to his ' white lock ;' said it was an inheritance in the family for several generations. He wore a slouch hat ; and I have watched him on several occasions, before the mirror, where he remained for a long time, arranging it on his curly hair for the best effect before starting for the Florian café.

"And this reminds me that he was in need sometimes of the wherewithal to procure his coffee. So he called on me for aid. It was amusing to me, for I had scarcely soldi to pay for my own, and so I often went without. However, I could well afford to pay for Whistler's coffee, inasmuch as he was a fine linguist, and I called on him to assist me in the battle I had with the padrona on two occasions. The mercenary woman was completely nonplussed, for Whistler waxed eloquent in the Italian tongue. There was no mistake, he was in dead earnest, for his gesticulations and excited tones of voice assured it, and my case was won.

"Tintoretto was his ideal artist among the old masters, and he often spoke most highly of his productions, especially ' The Crucifixion.'

"In the line of pastels he was original, doing them on ordinary wrapping-paper. They were simply beautiful. I saw them in a London gallery a few months later, and they were an inspiration ; so much so that he has had since many imitators but no equals.

"On one occasion I had a demonstration. We set out together on a sketching tour of the town. We came suddenly upon a subject that was very rich in tone—a cooper-shop.

RECOLLECTIONS AND IMPRESSIONS

I lost no time getting to work. I threw my sketching-block flat upon the pavement, and emptied the contents of my box of water-colors upon it to get the tone quickly. The paper being well saturated with water, made it an easy matter to bring forth light from out the deep tone with strips of blotting-paper. I was not aware of doing anything unusual until I heard a 'Ha, ha, ha!' which has been called Whistler's Satanic laugh.

"'What amuses you, Mr. Whistler? Why do you laugh? Are you making fun of my sketch?'

"'Oh, no,' said he, with assurance. 'I am admiring the ingenious way in which you work.'

"This to me was high praise, for it came from one who rarely indulged in praise."

Another, speaking of the same period, says :[1]

"I first knew Mr. James McNeill Whistler many years ago in Venice, when he was quite unknown to fame. He had lodging at the top of an old palace in the uttermost parts of the town, and many days he would breakfast, lunch, and dine off nothing more nutritious than a plateful of polenta or macaroni. He was just as witty, and gave himself just the same outrageous but inoffensive airs as afterwards in the days of his prosperity. He used to go about and do marvellous etchings for which he could find no market, or else only starvation prices. When he was absolutely obliged to, he would sell them for what he could get ; but he never lost the fullest confidence in his own powers ; and, whenever he could, he preferred to keep them in the expectation—nay, certainty—of being able to sell them some day at a high figure.

"He used to go roaming about Venice in search of sub-

---

[1] *McClure's Magazine*, vol. vii. p. 374.

jects for his etchings, and those who know all about it say
that the charm of his work lies quite as much in the choice
of subjects as in their execution.   He used to make a great
deal of mystery about his etching expeditions, and was
rarely prevailed upon to let any one accompany him.   If
he did, it was always under the strictest pledge of secrecy.
What was the use, he would ask, of his ferreting out some
wonderful old bridge or archway, and thinking of making it
immortal, if some second-rate painter-man were to come
after him and make it commonplace with his caricatures?
On the other hand, if some friend of his discovered an ideal
spot, and asked what he thought of it, he would not scruple
for an instant to say, 'Come, now, this is all nonsense, your
trying to do this.   It is much too good a subject to be wasted
on you.   You'd better let me see what I can do with it.'
And he would be so charming about it, and take his own
superiority so completely for granted, that no one ever
dreamed of refusing him.''

The story is told that a woman, some elderly
countess, moved into an apartment immediately
below him.   By her noise, fussiness, and goings to
and fro she annoyed him very much, and Whistler
wished her out.

The weather was hot, and one day the countess
put a jar of goldfish on the balcony immediately
beneath his window.   During her absence Whistler
tied a bent pin to a thread and caught the fish,
broiled them to a turn, and dropped them back.
Soon the countess returned, and on finding her
goldfish dead, there was a great commotion, and the
next day she packed up and left, saying that Venice
was altogether too hot,—the sun had cooked her
goldfish in their jar.

RECOLLECTIONS AND IMPRESSIONS

Of Whistler's etchings Seymour Haden once said that if he had to part with his Rembrandts or his Whistlers he would let the former go.

This collection of Haden's came to this country a few years ago.

An enthusiastic collector says :

"I should say of Mr. Whistler that he was an artistic genius, whose etched work has not been surpassed by any one, and equalled only by Rembrandt. Comparing the etching of the two, it should be said of Rembrandt that he chose greater subjects,—as, for instance, 'Christ Healing the Sick' and 'The Crucifixion ;' in landscape 'The Three Trees ;' and in portraiture 'Jan Lutma,' 'Ephraim Bonus,' and 'The Burgomaster Six.' It certainly cannot be said of Whistler that he ever etched any plates such as the two first mentioned. Though Rembrandt's etchings number, say, two hundred and seventy plates, when a buyer has bought fifty, he has, no matter how much money he may possess, all the Rembrandts he wants. In other words, two hundred and twenty plates are of little value.

"Whistler has catalogued three hundred and seventy-two plates ; but it would not do to think of stopping the buying of his prints with fifty, or twice that number, or any other figures, indeed, short of them all. The difference between Rembrandt and Whistler might be expressed in this way : Rembrandt etched many things whose technique was not the best, whose subjects were abominable, and whose work generally was far from pleasing. Whistler, on the contrary, has never etched a plate that would not be a delight to any connoisseur.

"I have fifty-five Rembrandts, and, with the exception of half a dozen more, I have all that I want, or all that I would buy, no matter how much money I had. Of Whistlers I have fifty-one, and I carry constantly in my pocket a list of as many more that I would be glad to buy if I had the chance. I can add that if I succeed in getting the others I shall then want as many more.

"While Whistler has not equalled Rembrandt in some of the great things, yet his average is very much higher. The latter etched scores of plates that do his memory no honor ; the former, on the contrary, has never etched one that will not be remembered with pleasure. To etch a fine portrait is the surest proof of the master ; the human face is the grandest subject that any artist ever had. I have always thought that Rembrandt's 'Jan Lutma' was the grand old man of all etched portraiture, though it is hard to see in what possible respect it surpasses 'The Engraver,' 'Becquet,' 'Drouet,' and other portraits by Whistler.

"Rembrandt's 'Three Trees,' in landscape, is a greater plate than Whistler's 'Zaandam,' though the latter is well-nigh perfection. I know no Rembrandt interior that approaches Whistler's 'Kitchen,' and I know no exteriors, unless possibly a few by Meryon, that approach his 'Palaces,' 'The Doorway,' 'Two Doorways,' the 'Embroidered Curtain,' and a score or two of others that are well known to all lovers of black and white.

"This story was started on Whistler ten or twelve years ago, and has been on its travels ever since : Some one asked him which of his etchings he thought the best. His answer was, 'All of them.' And he told the truth. Of plates that he thought much of, when I saw him thirteen years ago, the little 'Marie Loches,' which is another name for the Mayor's residence, was hung over his desk, and I distinctly remember that the fine 'Pierrot,' in the Amsterdam set, was also a prime favorite of his. Later I have heard it said that the portrait of 'Annie' he regarded as his finest figure piece."

In February, 1883, he exhibited in London, in the rooms of the Fine Arts Society, fifty-one etchings and dry-points.

It was, according to the placards,—and in reality,

RECOLLECTIONS AND IMPRESSIONS

—an "Arrangement in Yellow and White," for the room was white, with yellow mouldings ; the frames of the prints white, the chairs white, the ottomans yellow ; the draperies were yellow, with white butterflies ; there were yellow flowers in yellow Japanese vases on the mantels ; and even the attendants were clothed in white and yellow. As a French artist remarked, "It was a dream of yellow."

This, however, is how it struck some of the angry critics, who were impaled in the catalogue :

"While Mr. Whistler's staring study in yellow and white was open to the public we did not notice it,—for notice would have been advertisement, and we did not choose to advertise him.

"Of the arrangement in yellow and white, we note that it was simply an insult to the visitors,—almost intolerable to any one possessing an eye for color, which Mr. Whistler, fortunately for him, does not,—and absolutely sickening (in the strictest sense of the word) to those at all sensitive in such matters. 'I feel sick and giddy in this hateful room,' remarked a lady to us after she had been there but a few minutes. Even the common cottage chairs, painted a coarse yellow, did not solace the visitors ; and the ornaments on the mantel-piece, something like old bottle-necks, only excited a faint smile in the sickened company." [1]

The sea-sick lady was probably an invention of the writer.

Another, apparently somewhat less susceptible to the "sickening" effects of yellow, simply says :

---

[1] *Knowledge*, April 5, 1883, p. 208.

OF JAMES A. McNEILL WHISTLER

" Mr. Whistler has on view at the Fine Art Society's some half-a-hundred etchings ; but it was not to see these only that he invited his friends, and many fine people besides, last Saturday. In the laudable effort for a new sensation, he had been engaging in literature ; and a grave servant, dressed in yellow and white (to suit the temporary decoration of the walls during the show) pressed into the hands of those who had come in all innocence to see the etchings a pamphlet in which Mr. Whistler's arrangements had extended to an arrangement of critics." [1]

The catalogue which stirred the ire of the critics was an innocent little thing in brown-paper cover containing a list of the prints ; but beneath each was a line or two from the critics, and they were all there in outspoken condemnation of the work of the man who is now placed, by even the critics, on a plane with Rembrandt. Some have since confessed their errors in print and begged for the mantle of charity.

On the title-page appeared :

" Out of their own mouths shall ye judge them."

And here, as an example, is what he printed beneath " No. 51, Lagoon ; Noon." In mercy the names of the critics are omitted.

" Years ago James Whistler was a person of high promise."

" What the art of Mr. Whistler yields is a *tertium quid*."

" All of which gems, I am sincerely thankful to say, I cannot appreciate."

" As we have hinted, the series does not represent any Venice that we much care to remember ; for who wants to

---

[1] *The Academy*, February 24, 1883, p. 139.

RECOLLECTIONS AND IMPRESSIONS

remember the degradation of what has been noble, the foulness of what has been fair?"

"Disastrous failures."

"Failures that are complete and failures that are partial."

"A publicity rarely bestowed upon failures at all."

Whereupon Whistler brought the catalogue to a close with these scriptural sentences :

"Therefore is judgment far from us, neither doth justice overtake us ; we wait for light, but behold obscurity ; for brightness, but we walk in darkness."

"We grope for the wall like the blind, and we grope as if we had no eyes ; we stumble at noonday as in the night."

"We roar all, like bears."

Whistler's manner of arraigning his critics was his own. No one else could compile such delightful bits of literature as were those catalogues he issued from time to time ; but the idea of publishing adverse criticism with the work criticised was not new.

To his first edition of "Sartor Resartus" Carlyle— Whistler's neighbor in Chelsea—printed as an appendix the letter of condemnation which Murray the publisher received from his literary adviser and which led to the rejection of the manuscript.

The scheme is not without advantages,—it amuses the reader and confounds the critic, to which ends books and paintings are created.

How the galled jades winced may be gathered from the following mild comments:

"Mr. Whistler's catalogue, however, is our present game. He takes for motto, 'Who breaks a butterfly upon a wheel?'

OF JAMES A. McNEILL WHISTLER

But Mr. Whistler mistakes his vocation. He is no butterfly. He might be compared, perhaps, to a bird,—the bird that can sing but won't. If one judged, however, from some of his etchings, one would say a spider was nearer his mark. But a butterfly ! the emblem of all that is bright and beautiful in form and color ! Daniel Lambert might as reasonably have taken the part of the Apothecary in ' Romeo and Juliet,' or Julia Pastrana have essayed the *rôle* of Imogen.

" Criticism *is* powerless with him in many different ways. It is powerless to correct his taste for wilfully drawing ill. If a school-girl of ten showed such a picture of a human being as this (referring to illustration), for instance, we might criticise usefully enough. We might point out that no human being (we suppose the thing is intended for a human being, but it may be meant for a rag-bag) ever had such features or such shape. But of what use would it be to tell Mr. Whistler as much ? He knows it already, only he despises the public so much that he thinks it will do well enough for them.

" Again, criticism is powerless to explain what was meant by some such figure as this, in No. 33. The legs we can especially answer for, while the appendages which come where a horse has his feet and pasterns are perfect transcripts—they are things we never could forget. We have not the faintest idea what they really are. We would not insult Mr. Whistler by supposing he tried to draw a horse with the customary equine legs, and so failed as to produce these marvels. Perhaps Dr. Wilson knows of some animal limbed thus strangely.

" It is because of such insults as these to common sense and common understanding, and from no ill-will we bear him, that we refuse seriously to criticise such work as Mr. Whistler has recently brought before the public. Whatever in it is good adds to his offence, for it shows the offence to be wilful, if not premeditated." [1]

---

[1] *Knowledge*, April 6, 1883, pp. 208, 209.

RECOLLECTIONS AND IMPRESSIONS

Poor etchings,—condemned for their virtues, condemned for their faults,—there is no health in them.

And these and many similar things were written, only twenty years ago, of the greatest etchings the world has known since the days of Rembrandt.

When one thinks of the obscurity of Rembrandt to the day of his death, and how little his work was known for long after, of the passing of Meryon without recognition, it must be conceded that Whistler is coming into his own amazingly fast.

Senefelder discovered the process, but Whistler perfected the art of lithography. It was not until 1877, twenty years after he began etching, that he made his first lithographs.

There had been many before him, but none like him.

During the first half of the century the process was in great vogue in France, and men like Ingres, Millet, Corot, and Delacroix tried the facile stone.

One can readily understand how so fascinating a process appealed to Whistler, and the wonder is that he did not attempt it earlier.

The use of transfer-paper, whereby the artist is enabled to make his drawing when and where he pleases upon the paper, instead of being hampered by the heavy stone, has greatly advanced the art, though drawing on the stone possesses certain advantages and attractions over the paper.

OF JAMES A. McNEILL WHISTLER

Not many years ago Whistler was called as an expert witness in a case which involved the question whether the use of transfer-paper was lithography. The result of the case is of no consequence. While on the stand, he turned to the judge, and said :

"May I be permitted to explain, my lord, to these gentlemen (the jury) why we are all here?"

"Certainly not," answered the court ; "we are all here because we cannot help it."

The witty ruling of the court deprived those present of remarks which would have been not only to the point but greatly amusing.

It was in this case that an artist who had written many fine things about Whistler and his work appeared as a witness on the other side, and in cross-examining the great painter, counsel called attention to one of the complimentary things that had been written ("Mr. Whistler's almost nothings are priceless"), and asked, "You don't dissent to that, do you, Mr. Whistler?"

Whistler smiled, and replied, "It is very simple and very proper that Mr. —— should say that sort of a thing, but I attach no importance to it."

And it is really true that no man ever enjoyed more having nice things said about his work, and no man ever attributed less importance to either favorble or unfavorable comments. He accepted both as a matter of course and of no consequence ; neither he nor his work was affected in the slightest degree.

RECOLLECTIONS AND IMPRESSIONS

In 1896 he exhibited some seventy lithographs in the rooms of the Fine Arts Society, and they were a revelation of the possibilities of the process in the hands of a master of line.

The Way catalogue, now out of print, contained one hundred and thirty, purporting to cover those printed down to and including 1896.

To this list must be added at least eight more which are well known, and possibly others.

There are, therefore, in existence nearly four hundred etchings and dry-points by Whistler, and probably not less than one hundred and fifty lithographs, —a large volume of work for one man, even if he produced nothing else.

Stress is here laid upon the mere volume of his work to meet some remarkable views which have been put forth concerning him and to correct the popular impression that his controversies diverted him from his art.

He was but sixty-nine when he died. His first etchings appeared in 1857–58. For the remainder of his life he averaged twelve plates and lithographs a year,—one a month ; and of this great number, it is conceded by conservative experts, the percentage of successful plates and stones is much larger than that of any of his great predecessors. In fact, there are no failures. Some of the plates were more sketchy and of slighter importance than others, but every one is the genuine expression of the artist's mood at the moment of execution, and precious accordingly.

OF JAMES A. McNEILL WHISTLER

Not many years ago there was in a certain city an exhibition of the slight but pretty work of a famous French illustrator. By his grace, and especially by his happy facility in the drawing of children in checked frocks and gray or brown or blue stockings and stubby shoes, the work attracted attention, and, as always happens with the pretty and the novel, aroused an enthusiasm quite out of proportion to its real merit.

Two men fell into a dispute over the merits of the little drawings, one siding with the throng and maintaining they were great, the other insisting they were simply pretty,—too pretty to be good and really quite hard and mechanical in execution,—in fact, quite inconsequential as art.

"Look," said he, "at this figure of a child. See how the outline is painfully traced in black and then the colors filled in as mechanically and methodically as if a stencil had been used. What would a Jap say to that?"

"He would say it is fine. It is Japanese in color and motive."

"About as Japanese as a colored illustration in a modern magazine." The discussion became heated.

Oddly enough, at that moment a Japanese expert, who was crossing the country on his way to Europe to catalogue some collections, entered the room, and he was appealed to for his opinion of the drawing in question. In broken English he said :

"It is—very—pretty, very pretty ; but—I not know how you say it,—but it is what you call—

Spencerian,—yes, that is the name of the copy-
books—Spencerian writing, while a Japanese drawing is the—autograph—that is the difference—the
autograph."

And that is the difference between some of the
work of even the great ones before him and whatever Whistler did,—everything he touched was his
autograph ; whereas with even Rembrandt there is
the feeling now and then, though seldom, of the set
purpose, of the determination to secure a certain
result, of the intention to do something for others.
Whistler never did anything for any one but himself.
He never touched needle or brush to please model,
sitter, or patron.   Whenever the work in hand
ceased to amuse and interest him as a creation of his
own fancy, he dropped it.   He could not work after
his interest had evaporated.

There is in existence a water-color[1] bearing
Whistler's signature on the back, and also this
endorsement : "From my window.   This was his
first attempt at water-color.—E. W. Godwin."

It is a characteristic view of the Thames with Old
Battersea Bridge reaching almost from side to side.

In his pastels and water-colors, as in his etchings
and lithographs, he never forced a delicate medium
beyond its limitations.

Of all artists who ever lived, Whistler made the
least mystery of his art.

---

[1] Owned by Frank Gair Macomber, Esq., of Boston.

OF JAMES A. McNEILL WHISTLER

He not only expressed his intentions fully in his art, but also in unmistakable language.

In the first of his " Propositions," published many years ago, he laid down certain fundamental principles which controlled his use of etching, watercolor, and pastel, the first proposition being :

"That in art it is criminal to go beyond the means used in its exercise."

And he defined the limits of the etcher's plate, and by implication the dimensions of the watercolor and pastel—art's most fragile means.

In the famous " Propositions No. 2" he formulated the principles which governed his work as a painter, the first being :

"A picture is finished when all trace of the means used to bring about the end has disappeared."

And the last :

" The masterpiece should appear as the flower to the painter,—perfect in its bud as in its bloom,—with no reason to explain its presence, no mission to fulfil, a joy to the artist, a delusion to the philanthropist, a puzzle to the botanist, an accident of sentiment and alliteration to the literary man." [1]

These two sets of " Propositions," read in connection with his one lecture, the "Ten o'Clock," which was delivered in London, February 20, 1885,

---

[1] Gentle Art, p. 116.

at Cambridge, March 24, and Oxford, April 30, contain his creed in art.

Many a painter has written books explanatory of his art, but none has ever stated so plainly and so tersely the principles which actually governed all he did. Whistler was so epigrammatic in utterance that he was not taken seriously, but accused of paradox. But whoever reads what he has so soberly and earnestly said will better understand his work.

And whatever may be thought of reprinting entire the " Gentle Art," there can be no question about the great need of scattering broadcast the " Propositions" and the "Ten o'Clock."

OF JAMES A. McNEILL WHISTLER

V

*Chelsea—The Royal Academy—" Portrait of His
Mother"—" Carlyle"—Grosvenor Gallery—The
" Peacock Room"—Concerning Exhibitions.*

AFTER—possibly because—his "White Girl" was
rejected at the Salon, he went to London and made
his home at Chelsea, where he had as neighbors
Carlyle, Rossetti, George Eliot, and others of note
in art and literature.

Carlyle's description of Chelsea as it was in 1834,
when he and his wife moved there, is interesting,—
for the place changed little before Whistler came.
Writing to his wife concerning the house he had
found, Carlyle said :

"The street runs down upon the river, which I suppose
you might see by stretching out your head from the front
window, at a distance of fifty yards on the left. We are
called 'Cheyne Row' proper (pronounced *Chainie* Row), and
are a 'genteel neighborhood;' two old ladies on one side,
unknown character on the other, but with 'pianos.' The
street is flag pathed, sunk storied, iron railed, all old-fashioned and tightly done up ; looks out on a rank of sturdy
old *pollarded* (that is, beheaded) lime-trees, standing there
like giants in *tawtie* wigs (for the new boughs are still
young) ; beyond this a high brick wall ; backwards a garden,
the size of our back one at Comely Bank, with trees, etc., in
bad culture ; beyond this green hayfields and tree avenues,

once a bishop's pleasure-grounds, an unpicturesque yet rather cheerful outlook.   The house itself is eminent, antique, wainscoted to the very ceiling, and has been all new painted and repaired ; broadish stair with massive balustrade (in the old style), corniced and as thick as one's thigh ; floors thick as a rock, wood of them here and there worm-eaten, yet capable of cleanness, and still with thrice the strength of a modern floor.   And then as to rooms, Goody !   Three stories beside the sunk story, in every one of them three apartments, in depth something like forty feet in all—a front dining-room (marble chimney-piece, etc.), then a back dining-room or breakfast-room, a little narrower by reason of the kitchen stairs ; then out of this, and narrower still (to allow a back window, you consider), a china-room or pantry, or I know not what, all shelved and fit to hold crockery for the whole street.   Such is the ground area, which, of course, continues to the top, and furnishes every bedroom with a dressing-room or second bedroom ; on the whole a most massive, roomy, sufficient old house, with places, for example, to hang, say, three dozen hats or cloaks on, and as many crevices and queer old presses and shelved closets (all tight and new painted in their way) as would gratify the most covetous Goody,—rent, thirty-five pounds !   I confess I am strongly tempted.   Chelsea is a singular heterogeneous kind of spot, very dirty and confused in some places, quite beautiful in others, abounding with antiquities and the traces of great men,—Sir Thomas More, Steele, Smollett, etc.   Our row, which for the last three doors or so is a street, and none of the noblest, runs out upon a ' Parade' (perhaps they call it), running along the shore of the river, a broad highway with huge shady trees, boats lying moored, and a smell of shipping and tar.   Battersea Bridge (of wood) a few yards off ; the broad river, with white-trowsered, white-shirted Cockneys dashing by like arrows in thin, long canoes of boats ; beyond, the green, beautiful knolls of Surrey, with their villages,—on the whole a most artificial, green-painted, yet

lively, fresh, almost opera-looking business, such as you can
fancy. Finally, Chelsea abounds more than any place in
omnibi, and they take you to Coventry Street for sixpence.
Revolve all this in thy fancy and judgment, my child, and
see what thou canst *make* of it." [1]

Between Whistler and Rossetti there sprang up a
friendship that was singular, considering how diametrically opposite they were to one another in
nearly everything. They had, however, this in
common,—each was in search of a degree of the
beautiful quite beyond the grasp of the ordinary
mortal ; but of the two, Whistler's is incomparably
the finer art, for it is the purer and more abstract,
while Rossetti's painting exhibited the literary bent
very conspicuously,—it was inextricably involved
with his poetry.

One day he showed Whistler a sketch which
Whistler liked, and he urged Rossetti to go on with
it ; but Rossetti became so infatuated with his conception that instead of finishing the picture he wrote
a sonnet on the subject and read it to Whistler, who
said :

"Rossetti take out the picture and frame the
sonnet."

Life in Chelsea in those days had its drawbacks.

Whistler's utter lack of commercial instinct, his
dislike for the dealers, the habit he had of falling
out with any one who discussed money matters with
him, and that reluctance to part with pictures which

---

[1] Life of Carlyle, First Forty Years, vol. ii., pp. 345–6.

was a conspicuous trait through life, often involved him in trouble financially.

In 1879 E. W. Godwin designed and built for him a house in Tite Street.   It was of white brick, and known as the "White House," and is described as having been very artistic in so far as it was settled and furnished, but for some time only two rooms were in order.   "Everywhere you encountered great packing-cases full of pretty things, and saw preparations for papering and carpeting, but somehow or other nothing ever got any forwarder.   What was done was perfect in its way.   The white wainscoting, the rich draperies, the rare Oriental china, the pictures and their frames, the old silver, all had a charm and a history of their own." [1]

His powers of persuasion were such that it is said he once tamed a bailiff—temporarily in possession— to a degree of docility little short of amazing,—a favorite word of his.

"When the man first appeared he tried to wear his hat in the drawing-room and smoke about the house.   Whistler soon settled that.   He went out into the hall and fetched a stick, and daintily knocked the man's hat off.   The man was so surprised that he forgot to be angry, and within a day or two he had been trained to wait at table.   One morning, when Mr. Whistler was shaving, a message was brought up that the man (he was always known in the house as 'the man,' as if he were the only one of his species) wanted to speak to him.

[1] *McClure's Magazine*, vol. vii. p. 374.

OF JAMES A. McNEILL WHISTLER

" 'Very well, send him up,' said Mr. Whistler. He went on shaving, and when the man came in said, abruptly, 'Now, then, what do you want?'

" 'I want my money, sir.'

" 'What money?'

" 'My possession money, sir.'

" 'What, haven't they given it to you?'

" 'No, sir ; it's you that have to give it to me.'

" 'Oh, the deuce I have !' And Mr. Whistler laughingly gave him to understand that, if he wanted money, his only chance was to apply elsewhere.

" 'Well, I think it's very hard, sir,' the man began to snivel ; 'I have my own family to keep, and my own rent to pay——'

" 'I'll tell you what I advise you to do,' Mr. Whistler returned, as he gently pushed him out of the room : 'you should do as I do, and have "a man" in your own house.'

" Soon after this the man came and said that if he was not paid he would have to put bills up outside the house announcing a sale. And, sure enough, a few days after great posters were stuck up all over the front of the house, announcing so many tables, and so many chairs, and so much old Nankin china for sale on a given day. Mr. Whistler enjoyed the joke hugely, and hastened to send out invitations to all his friends to a luncheon-party, adding, as a postscript, 'You will know the house by the bills of sale stuck up outside.' And the bailiff proved an admirable butler, and the party one of the merriest ever known." [1]

The "White House" was finally sold, and it is said that when he moved out he wrote on the wall, "Except the Lord build the house, their labor is in vain that build it,—E. W. Godwin, R.S.A., built this one."

---

[1] *McClure's Magazine*, vol. vii. p. 374.

RECOLLECTIONS AND IMPRESSIONS

Speaking of architects, the story is told that he was once dining, and dining well, at the house of a friend in London. Towards the end of the dinner he was obliged to leave the table and run up-stairs to write a note. In a few moments a great noise was heard in the hall, and Whistler was found to have fallen down the stairs. "Who is your architect?" he asked. His host told him. "I might have known it; the —— teetotaler!"

By the irony of fate the "White House" was afterwards occupied and much altered by the detested critic of the *Times*,—detested possibly because he occupied and dared to alter the house,— and Whistler asked:

"Shall the birthplace of art become the tomb of its parasite?"

It was this critic who pronounced a water-color drawing of Ruskin by Herkomer the best oil portrait the painter had ever done,—a mistake Whistler never let the unlucky writer forget.

In those days he exhibited quite frequently at the Royal Academy.

Among the earliest pictures exhibited was "At the Piano." It attracted the attention of the Scotch painter John Phillip, who wished to buy it. Whistler left the price to him, and Phillip sent a check for thirty guineas, which was entirely satisfactory, so far as any one knows.

Thirty thousand dollars has already been paid for one of his very early pictures, and for any one of a

Arrangement in Gray and Black.
Portrait of the Painter's Mother

half-dozen of his important canvases a bid of fifty thousand dollars may be had any day.

It is a question of only a few years when Whistler's paintings will sell as high as Rembrandt's. The great galleries of Europe have not yet entered the field, and many of the great private collections have no example of his work. A few Americans, but not many out of the large number of those who buy pictures regardless of cost, are already inquiring. When all these factors come into competition, as they will soon or late, prices will be realized that will make the dearest of English or French painters seem cheap.

In 1872 the portrait of his mother, an "Arrangement in Gray and Black," was sent in to the Academy, and accepted only after a sharp controversy, wherein Sir William Boxall, R.A., gave the committee their choice between hanging the picture and accepting his own resignation as one of their number. "For," said he, "it shall never be told of me that I served on a committee which refused such a work as that." The picture was eventually placed with the "black-and-white" exhibit, drawings, engravings, etc., and apparently only the critics saw it. What they said Whistler has himself recorded.

Somebody has asked, Suppose Whistler had been taken up and made an A.R.A., and in due course an R.A.—what then?

The thing is well-nigh inconceivable ; and even if an A.R.A., his innate dislike for sham and preten-

sion in art and his sense of humor would have prevented him from becoming a full-fledged academi-
cian in a body wherein, as in all similar bodies,
mutual appreciation, or at least mutual restraint
from honest depreciation, is essential to existence.

Whistler would probably have accepted the first
degree, the A.R.A., of the fraternity,—for all his life
he was personally, but not in his art, singularly susceptible to the praise of his fellow-men ; but he
would have remained in the Academy about as long
as he remained president of the British Society of
Painters,—just long enough to overturn things generally, and then get out.

Once, when taken to task for referring to a painter
who was only an A.R.A. as an R.A., he retorted that
it was a difference without distinction.

To the orthodox academicians his work was a
mystery. Once, when dining in a restaurant in the
West End, the waiter, having difficulty in supplying
Whistler's wants, said, "Well, sir, I can't quite make
out what you mean."

"Gad, sir," he cried, in tones of amazement, "are
you an R.A. ?"

It is not within the range of possibilities that the
Royal Academy, or any other institution, would have
had any perceptible influence on Whistler's art,—on
that side he was indifferent to the influences which
affect most men, to considerations of gain and
popular appreciation.

In the account of a certain public sale the statement was printed that when one of his pictures was

put up it was loudly hissed.   He sat down and wrote the editor acknowledging the compliment, " the distinguished though unconscious compliment so publicly paid.   It is rare that recognition so complete is made during the lifetime of the painter."

Another time he said, "There are those, they tell me, who have the approval of the public, and live."

Long after he ceased to exhibit at the Academy a lady met him at one of the exhibitions, and expressed her surprise.

"Well, you know," he answered, "one must do something to lend interest to the show,—so here I am."

Years after, the Academy, while Leighton was president, invited him to send some of his pictures, and here is the account of what happened :[1]

" He was in Brussels.   There came a telegram from him to me which was a cry of exultation :

" ' MY DEAR S. : The Lord hath delivered them into my hands.   I am sending you by post their last dying confession.'

"And so next morning the post duly brought a letter from Whistler inclosing the official proposal from the Royal Academy, signed by Mr. Eaton, secretary to that distinguished body, inviting Whistler to contribute to a loan exhibition then presently to be held.   Whistler wrote :

" ' Of course, I refuse.   You know me too well to doubt that.   Do they think they can use me after so long trampling on me ?   Do they think I don't see what they want ?   Do

---

[1] G. W. Smalley, in the London *Times*.   Reprinted in the New York *Tribune*, August 19, 1903.

they think I need them? At last they perceive that they need me, but in the day of their extremity they shall ask in vain.'

"I am quoting from memory, but I give the substance accurately. He inclosed his answer to the Academy, long since a public document, with permission to cable it if I liked to America. I telegraphed Whistler begging him to send no answer till my letter should reach him. He wired: 'I do not understand, but I will wait till to-morrow.' I wrote to him in the best ink, as Merimee said, at my command. I tried to point out that the Academy had offered him the *amende honorable;* that their invitation was an acknowledgment of their error, and was meant as an atonement; that if he sought to humiliate his enemies, no humiliation could be so complete as their public surrender, of which the proof would be the hanging of his works on their walls, and much else which I thought obvious and conclusive. And I begged him to remember that I had always thought him right, and always said the world would come round to him, and that now, as ever before, whether right or wrong, mine was the counsel of a friend. The answer came by wire early next morning: 'Alas, my dear S., that you too should have gone over to the enemy!' I believe if I had but besought him to consider that his acceptance would have been a service to art, and if he could himself have thought that it would be, he would have accepted. I never saw Whistler again, never heard from him; a friendship of twenty years came there and then to an end—on his side.''

In 1897 a circular was mailed to him, addressed, "The Academy, England." At the post-office they added "Burlington House," where it was declined. Finally the circular reached him, bearing the endorsement, "Not known at the R. A." He gave it to the press, saying, "In these days of doubtful frequentation, it is my rare good fortune to be able to send you an unsolicited, official, and final certificate of character."

The fact was, mail addressed simply "Whistler, England," would reach him.

The Grosvenor Gallery, opened in 1877 by Sir Coutts Lindsay, offered an opportunity to many a man who either would not or could not exhibit at the Academy.

It was here that some of Whistler's best things were shown,—the portraits of Irving as Philip II. ; Miss Rosa Corder ; Miss Gilchrist, the actress ; the Carlyle ; Miss Alexander ; and Lady Archibald Campbell, commonly known as "The Lady with the Yellow Buskin," and many of his famous nocturnes.

Whistler had a very peculiar laugh,—demoniacal his enemies called it,—and it is said that while his portrait was being painted, Irving caught this laugh and used it with effect in the part of Mephistopheles, —but then, who knows ?

The story of the painting and the naming of "The Yellow Buskin" is worth repeating.

Lady Archibald Campbell was an exceedingly handsome woman, and Whistler expressed the desire to paint her portrait. She graciously consented, and the sittings began.

In those days Whistler was looked upon in London as little less than a mountebank in art, and one day, putting it as nicely as she could, she said :

" My husband wished me to say that he—he appreciated the honor of your inviting me to sit for a portrait, but that—that he did not wish to be understood as committing himself in any way, and the picture must not be considered a commission."

"Dear me, no," said Whistler, as he painted away ; "under no circumstances. Lord Archibald need give himself no uneasiness,—my compensation is in your condescension. We are doing this for the pleasure there is in it."

The portrait was finished, exhibited as "*La Dame au Brodequin Jaune*,"—and duly ridiculed.

Lady Campbell's friends expressed surprise that she should have permitted so eccentric an artist to do so ugly a thing. But time went on ; the picture made a profound sensation and won its way.

Some time after, Whistler met Lady Campbell in London, and she said to him :

"My dear Mr. Whistler, I hear my portrait has been exhibited everywhere and become famous."

"Sh—sh—sh !" with finger on lips. "So it has, my dear Lady Archibald ; but every discretion has been observed that Lord Campbell could desire,— your name is not mentioned. The portrait is known as 'The Yellow Buskin.'"

It is now in the Wilstach collection, in Philadelphia.

Whistler preferred to exhibit his work under conditions which he controlled. As early as 1874 he gave a special exhibition in London, and in the years 1880, 1881, 1883, 1884, and 1886 he exhibited

Arrangement in Black.
La Dame au Brodequine Jaune

either prints or paintings in the rooms of the Fine
Arts Society.

He always occupied the place of honor with the
International Society at Knightsbridge.

Occasionally he would use the galleries of dealers,
but not often, and then only upon his own terms.

While living at Chelsea he had Carlyle as a near
neighbor, and of his own notion he painted the portrait that now hangs in Glasgow.

These two extraordinary beings were quite congenial. The dogmatic old philosopher, then past sev-
enty-five, sat day after day to the eccentric painter,
who was nearly forty years his junior, as patiently as
if he were a professional model, and the sittings were
long and tedious.

One day, as he was leaving, quite exhausted, he
met at the door a little girl in white, and he asked
her name.

"I am Miss Alexander," she said, primly, "and I
am going to have my portrait painted."

The sage shook his head in commiseration, and
muttered, as he passed on :

"Puir lassie, puir lassie !"

If proof were required of the underlying sincerity
and earnestness of Whistler in those days when the
world refused to take him seriously, this long and
intimate association with Carlyle would be more than
sufficient.

They were neighbors. Carlyle had every opportunity of seeing Whistler on the street and in his

studio. Seemingly two beings could not be less sympathetic, and yet the philosopher who had so few good words for any one, who was the implacable foe of sham and falsehood, who was intolerant of the society of others, who cared little for art and less for artists, freely gave his time and society to the most unpopular painter in England.

In truth there was a good deal in common between the two,—in the attitude of the one towards literature and what his fellow-writers were saying, and in the attitude of the other towards art and what his fellow-painters were doing. Each stood in his own sphere for the highest ideals, and no doubt each recognized in the other the quality of sincerity in his profession.

Poor Carlyle! your name should never be mentioned without an anathema for the scavengers who dealt with your memory. If they are not suffering the torments of the damned, the mills of the gods have ceased to turn.

Froude prefaced the Life of Carlyle with a long protestation that it contained the truth, the whole truth, and nothing but the truth; which, it seems, according to even his notions, was a lie; for in the secrecy of his closet he prepared a pamphlet containing the revelations of the Jewsbury creature,— the expert opinion of "an ill-natured old maid," as Mrs. Carlyle called her,—to the effect that Carlyle should never have married; and this pamphlet, containing the salacious tittle-tattle between himself and

Arrangement in Gray and Black.
Portrait of Thomas Carlyle

this old maid, is given the world as presumably his last instalment of revelations, though no one knows how much similar stuff the Jewsbury creature, a romancer by profession, may have left pigeon-holed for still further harm.

And the answer to it all is that Carlyle, in spite of the old maid's opinion, was married ; and what is more to the point, remained married forty years, with no more of differences and dissensions, even accepting all the Froude-Jewsbury tattle, than any good wife will have with any good Scotchman ; and during their long married life she was a help and an inspiration to her husband, and after her death she was mourned as few wives in the history of mankind have been mourned.

A depth beyond the imagination of Dante must be found for the Froude-Jewsbury combination.

As the portrait neared completion, Carlyle took a good look at it one day, seemed pleased, and said :

"Weel, man, you have given me a clean collar, and that is more than Meester Watts has done."

The portrait was begun and ended as a labor of love, and for nearly twenty years it remained unsold.

After Carlyle died some citizens of Glasgow, from purely patriotic motives, and with no appreciation whatsoever of the painting, thought it should be purchased, and a public subscription was started.

When the amount first talked of—quite a small sum—had been nearly subscribed, Whistler learned that the subscription paper expressly disavowed all approval of himself and his art, whereupon he promptly more than doubled the price, to the dismay of the canny Scots, who wished to buy the portrait without the art ; and when they hesitated, he again raised the price, to their utter discomfiture, and the picture was not purchased until 1891.

It is now owned by the corporation of Glasgow, and hangs in the public gallery surrounded by a mass of lesser works which completely dwarf its great proportions and render adequate appreciation impossible.

It is worth while to visit Glasgow to see this portrait, but until the authorities have the good judgment to give it a room, or at least a wall to itself, the journey will prove an exasperation.

The hanging of pictures is a "lost art ;" and most of the art of pictures is lost in the hanging.

A picture is painted in a certain environment of light, color, and tone,—and to Whistler this environment was a vital consideration. For the time being the canvas is the one conspicuous thing in the studio, of even greater importance than subject or model. From this environment of creation, and with which it is in perfect harmony, it is violently forced into conjunction with great squares of atrocious gilt frames and expanses of clashing canvases.

A gallery of pictures is the slaughter-house of art ; annual exhibitions are the shambles of beauty.

So far as galleries are concerned, the advantage is usually with the dealer, for he knows the value of arrangement and shows his best things more or less detached. One by one the gems of his collection are presented to the customer and time given for appreciation.

There are but two uses to which a painting can be put with any sense of the fitness of things : it may be used decoratively alone or in connection with one or two others which harmonize and which are distributed to produce a perfect effect ; this is the noblest use to which a painting of any kind can be put, the production of an effect in which the painting, however great, is but an element in a perfect whole.

Another and commoner use is the enjoyment of a picture by itself, as one reads a poem or listens to music, more or less oblivious to all surroundings. It is obvious that this sort of enjoyment implies the subordination of all surroundings to the painting, or the poem, or the music, the arrangement of the environment so as to secure the greatest possible freedom from intrusive and distracting sights and sounds,—in short, as regards painting, the reproduction in a sense of the atmosphere of the studio where the picture was created, or of the place, altar, or chapel for which it was intended ; and it means most emphatically freedom from sharp contrast with pictures by other men and of other times, schools, and conditions, however good, which will clash precisely as would two orchestras playing different pieces in the same hall.

RECOLLECTIONS AND IMPRESSIONS

One can imagine Whistler and Carlyle—painter and philosopher, two masters, each in his vocation—in the studio, and the growing portrait, a thing of beauty *there*, a bond of union between two men so divergent, and one can imagine how beautiful the portrait would be anywhere if by itself amidst harmonious surroundings, whether used as the chief ornament of a dignified hall or placed in a more neutral atmosphere for study and appreciation. But one cannot imagine more destructive surroundings than those of a public gallery, the walls of which teem with writhing, wriggling things in huge gilt frames and glaring colors.

And the painters, who ought to know better, but who encourage these great collections and exhibitions, who live for them, work for them, slave for them, are more to blame for the existence of these heterogeneous conglomerations than the public, who do not know better, but walk helplessly about amidst endless rows of staring canvases, dimly conscious that all is not right.

Pictures of equal merit do not necessarily hang together. A Valesquez and a Raphael, each supremely beautiful in the place for which it is intended, produce an inharmonious effect if placed side by side.

A rabble, with men or pictures, is a throng composed of more or less incongruous and unsympathetic units.

With the exception of the few instances, as in

the Turner room in the National Gallery in London, where the works of one man are grouped for the express purpose of comparison and study, every collection of pictures is a rabble, and as a whole —ugly.

Nor does the grouping of the works of one man in one room produce a beautiful effect, a beautiful room ; not at all, for they are grouped for a scientific rather than an æsthetic purpose, for the purpose of study and comparison in a room which is, as it should be, otherwise barren and neutral.

One or, at most, two fine pictures are all any ordinary room will stand, and to produce an effect wherein nothing overwhelmingly predominates, but everything finds its place and remains there, re-quires genius different from but of the same high order as that of the painter, and that sort of genius has been lacking in the Western world for some centuries.

So low has the once great art of painting fallen that it has helplessly relinquished its original field of great achievement, the adornment of buildings inside and out, and that has become a separate trade so incompetently followed that the phrase " interior decorator" is one of reproach.

And yet little as the commercial " interior dec-orator" knows about decoration, it is safer to trust to his fustian stock of burlaps, wall-papers, imitation leathers, metals, lustres, and illuminations than follow the guidance of the painters themselves,—for, with rare exceptions, they know nothing beyond the

RECOLLECTIONS AND IMPRESSIONS

narrow confines of their frames, and their own houses and studios resemble curiosity-shops.

The art of decoration, which implies the co-op-eration of architect, sculptor, and painter as a unit, has not been practised since the sixteenth century, and not in any high degree of perfection since three hundred years before.

With the disintegration of the union among the arts, each has accomplished endless detached and isolated perfections, but nothing that is really worth while in the sense that a Greek temple or a Gothic cathedral was worth while,—for nothing so chaste and perfect as the former or so sublime and beau-tiful as the latter has been done since each of the three constructive arts began to work in jealous in-dependence of the others.

Rossetti and Whistler were both friends of the wealthy and eccentric ship-owner F. R. Leyland, of No. 50 Prince's Gate. He was a collector of things rare and beautiful, a "patron" of art and artists, a musician, and altogether a character one associates with Romance rather than with London.

It was for him that Whistler painted the famous "Peacock Room," under the following circum-stances :

Leyland had bought the "Princess of the Land of Porcelain," and one day Whistler went to see it in place. He found it in a dining-room which was richly decorated with costly Spanish leather and a heavy ceiling of wood, a place altogether too sombre

for his bright and brilliant " Princess," and he pro-
tested against the discord.

"What would you do ?" asked Leyland.

" Paint the room."

"What ! paint that beautiful Spanish leather?"

" Most assuredly,—if this is to be the boudoir of
the ' Princess.' "

Whistler was told to go ahead and make the room
harmonize with the painting.

He started in and covered every inch of wall
surface, even the insides of the shutters, with a wonderful scheme of decoration in blue and gold, the
brilliant coloring of the peacock, making a color-
effect rich beyond description.

Unhappily, nothing had been said concerning the
price, and that finally named by Leyland seemed to
Whistler quite inadequate ; but he made no com-
plaint and went on with the work. The trouble
came when Leyland paid in pounds instead of
in guineas. That was more than Whistler could
stand.

All professional men in England being paid in
guineas, he would not permit art to be dealt with as
merchandise. He felt, therefore, that he had been
robbed of his shillings, and the whole affair, which
from the beginning had been a matter of pleasure
rather than of profit with him, was placed on a commercial footing. Considering the time spent, the
surface covered, the work done, the price fixed by
Leyland was quite inadequate. Then, to pay in scant

pounds, instead of full guineas, that was, in truth, adding insult to injury.

The work was not quite complete, and he took his revenge by painting his "patron" in the guise of a peacock, with his claws on what might be mere decoration, or, as any one might fancy, a pile of guineas. The likeness was not immediately perceptible, but, with a hint, the world soon saw it, and laughed.

Leyland has been dead a long time, and the house has passed from his family, but the "Peacock Room" is still in existence, and the curious visitor is occasionally, but not often, admitted. The "Princess" no longer hangs at one end, for long ago she went to Scotland, and will soon find her way to America; but the two peacocks are at the other end,—one the personification of the grasping "patron" and the other bearing a faint though perceptible likeness to the defiant painter with the white lock.

The shelves, which were once filled with the rarest of blue-and-white china, are now given over to books, and altogether the place is but a melancholy reminder of former beauty. But the decoration is in good condition, and could the walls and ceilings be removed and the "Princess" restored, the original effect would be reproduced.

The construction of the room was not Whistler's, so he worked under great disadvantages in dealing with architectural features, particularly the ceiling, which he did not like; so the room, if ever removed, would not represent his ideas of proportion and construction. It would simply show how he made the best of a difficult situation.

The architect who designed the room and looked upon the house as his stepping-stone to fame, when he saw the—to him—desecration, was completely unbalanced, went insane, and died not long after.

If opportunities had offered, Whistler would have been a great decorator, for such was his susceptibility to color that he could not tolerate discordant effects about him. It was ever his habit to decorate his studio, his house, or any rooms he occupied to suit his exceedingly fastidious taste.

He did not "decorate" in the sense the term is accepted nowadays. In truth, the casual visitor to his studio or to his house would depart under the impression there was no decoration at all, for neither figures nor patterns made the walls attractive, yet from floor to ceiling every square inch was a matter of extreme solicitude. He would mix colors and apply them with his own hands until the room was in harmony.

Even the great barn of an attic which was his studio in Paris was painted by him, so that from its dark—not black—rich oak floor, along base-boards and walls, to sloping roof, the effect was such as he sought as an environment for his pictures,—a brown, a grayish brown, a soft and singular shade of brown, hard to describe, difficult to see, but delightful to *feel* in its sober and retiring neutrality,—and that is the best color, the best tone, against which to hang

RECOLLECTIONS AND IMPRESSIONS

Whistler's paintings in any general exhibition, for it remains quietly and unobtrusively in the background, and at the same time the silvery quality in it gives it life.

When London laughed at his "Yellow and White" exhibition of etchings it did not know that a master of color was giving an object-lesson in interior decoration.

Who can recall without a feeling of restful satisfaction the delightful reception-room of that later home in Paris, at 110 Rue du Bac? So simple that, really, there was not a conspicuous feature about it, and yet every detail had been worked out with as much care as he bestowed on a painting.

This feature of Whistler's art, this susceptibility to color and line in surroundings will be referred to again in the discussion of his exquisite color-sense.

For the present it is sufficient to point out that he was something more than a painter of easel pictures ; that instinctively he was akin to those great masters who combined their efforts with those of the architect in the endeavor to produce beautiful results.

A sympathetic writer has said :

"Although he was in no way a spendthrift, he would make every sort of sacrifice to his art. Had he been given more opportunity, there seems no reason to doubt that he would have made other rooms even more beautiful than the famous 'Peacock' dining-room. But, frankly, the public did not care for his work enough to buy much of it from him at anything like a fair price ; so that he was obliged to limit himself to comparatively small surfaces, easel pictures, over

OF JAMES A. McNEILL WHISTLER

which collectors will soon begin to wrangle, we dare say, now that the clever hand which created them can work no more, and the big, kind heart which gave this man the cour- age to fight through fifty years against ' *la bêtise humaine*' is cold and still." [1]

In showing his work to visitors he exercised all the reserve and discretion of the Japanese, who places before his guests but one kakemona during that most formal and elaborate of social festivities, the "Tea Ceremony," or who, under pressure of re- peated requests, takes from its little box and unfolds from its many silken wrappings one, just one, of his precious bits of porcelain. No more on the same day, lest the surfeited guests fail in appreciation.

If in his studio, Whistler would first turn to the wall every picture and arrange the few pieces of fur- niture so that nothing should attract the vagrant eye, then he would place the one picture he wished seen on the easel in the best of light, without, however, letting it be seen until frame and glass were care- fully wiped, when, stepping back on a line with his visitor, he, too, would enjoy his work as if he saw it for the first time. He would never exhibit anything he was tired of, and he never tired of anything he exhibited. This appreciation of his own work, his enthusiasm over what he had done, was often mis- understood by people accustomed to the false mod- esty of artists who stand dumb while others vainly

---

[1] *Harper's Weekly*, August 1, 1903.

strive to see in their work the beauties which they of all people can best make known.

If time permitted he might bring forth two, or even three, pictures, but rarely more, and always each by itself. If some visitor, presuming on his good nature,—and he was indulgent in the extreme to those he liked,—insisted on placing the pictures side by side for comparison, as is the custom in shops, he was as uneasy and unhappy as would be a poet if several persons insisted on reading aloud before him several of his poems at the same time,— for what is a picture but a poem, mute to the ear but clarion-voiced to the eye?

In public exhibitions of his works he had the same sense of the eternal fitness of things.

First of all, the room must be properly lighted, and Whistler's paintings require a soft light. In his studio the skylight was well arranged with shades, so he could keep the light soft and constant; and frequently he would draw the shades so as to make the room quite dark, and then view portrait and sitter as they loomed up in shadow.

"Some students planned to call on him one New Year's morning. A friendly student, not at all sure that Whistler would like it, gave him a little tip as to the surprise party.

"'Tell them that I never receive callers,' he exclaimed, excitedly. The student explained that he wasn't supposed to know anything about it.

"'Are you sure they mean well?' he inquired, anxiously. And on being reassured, 'Well, tell them I never receive visitors in the morning.'

OF JAMES A. McNEILL WHISTLER

" The students called in the afternoon, and found awaiting them a most genial and delightful host. He told stories and showed them his palettes to prove that he practised what he preached, and pictures and sketches were exhibited to them never seen by the public, among the surprising ones being some allegorical studies. He served them with champagne and fruits and cakes, and was most solicitous as to their enjoyment. One of them asked him how he arranged his subjects so as to produce the low tone noted in his pictures. He posed a visitor, pulled over the shades so as to shut out all light, save from one window, and there before them was a living Whistler ' arrangement' ready to recede behind a frame, as he says all portraits should do."

It is a pity to ever subject his pictures to the trying light of the usual gallery, and it is a still greater pity to exhibit them at night in competition with foot-lights and foyer. His work should not be made the attraction for either a " five-o'clock tea" or a dress rehearsal. People who will not go during the day are not worth inviting.

The fact that people are content to view the best paintings of all time by artificial light, and even profess to find a " softness" and " charm" lacking by day, is but additional evidence of that want of susceptibility and fine feeling which characterizes the modern world, artists and laymen alike. For no picture that was painted by daylight should be seen at night, if all its beauties are to be felt.

A room for the exhibition of his pictures should be of precisely the right tone, and this is a matter of no little difficulty.

135

RECOLLECTIONS AND IMPRESSIONS

When president of the Society of British Artists, in 1886, his arrangement of the rooms was criticised as being "tentative," because he had left the battens on the walls ; whereupon he wrote that in the engineering of the light and the treatment of the walls and the arrangement of the draperies everything was intentional ; that the battens were meant to remain, "not only for their use, but as bringing parallel lines into play that subdivide charmingly the lower portions of the walls and add to their light appearance ; that the whole combination is complete."

There is a hint to all managers of exhibitions.

To summarize the foregoing suggestions :

The tone of the walls should be such as to keep them in the background.

The monotonous blankness of the walls may be broken by unobtrusive lines, not arbitrarily for effect, but justifiably for use and effect.

Only such draperies should be used as are absolutely necessary to reduce vacancies or to soften harsh lines, and these should lose themselves in the tone of the room.

Floor should be low in tone, the rich, dark brown of old oak keeping its place under foot best of all.

If the room is large and a few chairs and benches are admitted, they should be of wood, plain and for service alone, as becomes a room that is arranged but for one purpose,—namely, the exhibition of certain pictures,—and they should be painted or stained in tone to correspond with the room.

The light should be under absolute control, and kept quite soft, diffused, and constant throughout the day.

The room should be closed at night, or at least the people fully warned by notices in catalogue and elsewhere that if they have any real desire to see and understand the pictures they will come during the day.

The pictures should be well spaced, so that each may, to a certain degree, be studied by itself, for each is as complete a work as a piece of music.

In short, in an exhibition of pictures, or of anything else, everything should be subordinated to the things exhibited ; nothing should be permitted to obtrude upon the attention to their disadvantage ; the work of the decorator and furnisher on such an occasion is perfect when it is unnoticed.

For black-and-whites, experiments in color may be made, but for paintings which are compositions in color the background should be neutral,—silent like the background of music.

As every one knows, green and red, side by side, accentuate and help each other ; therefore, pictures in which the prevailing tone is green are helped by a red or crimson background, while pictures in which the prevailing tone is red are helped by a green background.

The foregoing is elementary and a matter of common observation, and the walls of art galleries

and exhibitions are frequently covered with either a
shade of green or a shade of crimson ; but in placing
pictures no discrimination is exercised,—landscapes
and marines in which green predominates are placed
side by side with portraits and interiors in which red
frequently predominates on the same green or red
background, to the advantage of one set of pictures
and the detriment of the other.

So far as color-effect is concerned, the pictures
themselves go very well side by side, the red of
the life pieces helping the green of the nature
pieces, and *vice versa ;* but if the background is
permitted to assert itself, if the pictures are spaced
on the wall, any background which accentuates the
one class does so at the expense of the other.

If pictures in which the prevailing tone is green
are to be placed on the same wall with pictures in
which red predominates, the background should be
neither red nor green, but, theoretically, a gray,
which is neutral and helps all colors in contrast ;
practically, however, a grayish hue of brown, because pure gray requires a greater expanse of wall
between each picture than the exigencies of an
exhibition or of a typical picture gallery permit,
while the element of brown permits the wall to
assert itself a little more positively between the
frames, and, at the same time, the quality of neutrality is almost as well preserved.

The stronger the tone of the background the
nearer together pictures may be placed ; the weaker
and more neutral the background the wider the

spacing must be,—a pure gray requiring the widest spacing of all backgrounds, a deep crimson the narrowest. In other words, it requires a wide expanse of gray to support a little color, while a very little crimson will carry a very large expanse of color in the way of gilt frames and strong landscapes and marines.

Wide frames, whether of gold or dark wood, enable green walls to carry green pictures and red walls to carry red pictures without the pictures suffering so much ; the frames intervene, and the immediate contrast is between canvas and frame instead of canvas and wall. But the secondary contrast is there and is felt precisely in proportion to the extent of the spacing between the pictures, and the pictures suffer accordingly.

RECOLLECTIONS AND IMPRESSIONS

VI

The Ruskin Suit—His Attitude towards the World and towards Art—"The Gentle Art of Making Enemies"—Critics and Criticism.

In 1877 Ruskin, passing through the Grosvenor Gallery, caught sight of something the like of which he had never seen in the world of art. It was the "Nocturne, Black and Gold. The Falling Rocket," a faithful transcript of the painter's impression of a night-scene in Cremorne Gardens. But Ruskin cared less for the subtle glories of night than for the more garish beauties of the day, and still less for the sights and sounds of Cremorne Gardens, and neither he nor any one else in either modern or ancient world knew anything at all about the painting of night as Whistler painted it. It is not surprising, therefore, that he was startled, for the picture seemed to violate all those canons of art which he had laid down in English the beauty of which more than condones his every error, and on the impulse of the moment he wrote in a number of *Fors Clavigera* :

"For Mr. Whistler's own sake, no less than for the protection of the purchaser, Sir Coutts Lindsay ought not to have admitted works into the gallery in which the ill-educated conceit of the artist so nearly

Nocturne, Black and Gold. The Falling Rocket

approached the aspect of wilful imposture. I have
seen and heard much of cockney impudence before
now, but never expected to hear a coxcomb ask two
hundred guineas for flinging a pot of paint in the
public's face.''

By way of extenuation, it must be borne in mind
that this was written off-hand, at a time when Ruskin
was saying so many extravagant things, though with
them so many profoundly true things, that no one
quite understood him, and many thought him not
quite sound mentally. The habit of sweeping gen-
eralizations, of extravagant appreciations and de-
preciations had grown apace since the publication
of the first volume of " Modern Painters," nearly
forty years before, and he invariably yielded to the
impression or the prejudice of the moment.

If Ruskin, in estimating Whistler, had paused but
a moment and recalled just a paragraph from the
preface to the second edition of the first volume of
" Modern Painters" he would have been more toler-
ant, for he there said :

  "All that is highest in art, all that is creative and im-
aginative, is formed and created by every great master for
himself, and cannot be repeated or imitated by others. We
judge of the excellence of a rising writer, not so much by
the resemblance of his works to what has been done before
as by their difference from it ; and while we advise him, in
the first trials of strength, to set certain models before him,
with respect to inferior points,—one for versification, another

RECOLLECTIONS AND IMPRESSIONS

for arrangement, another for treatment,—we yet admit not
his greatness until he has broken away from all his models
and struck forth versification, arrangement, and treatment of
his own.''

And was not Ruskin himself the life-long apolo-
gist for a most original and extraordinary genius,—
a man who to his last days was as little understood
as Whistler?

Here are some things that were said of Turner as
late as 1842, when he was doing some of his best
work :

''The 'Dogano' (*sic*) and 'Campo Santo' have a glorious
ensemble, and are produced by wonderful art, but they mean
nothing.   They are produced as if by throwing handfuls of
white and blue and red at the canvas, letting what chanced
to stick, stick, and then shadowing in some forms to make
the appearance of a picture ; and yet there is a fine harmony
in the highest range of color to please the sense of vision.
We admire and we lament to see such genius so employed.
But 'Farther on you may fare worse.'   No. 182 is a snow-
storm of most unintelligible character,—the snow-storm of a
confused dream, with a steamboat 'making signals,' and (apparently, like the painter who was in it) 'going by the head'
(lead ?).   Neither by land nor water was such a scene ever
witnessed.   And of 338, 'Burial at Sea,' though there is a
striking effect, still the whole is so idealized and removed
from truth that, instead of the feeling it ought to effect, it
only excites ridicule.   And No. 353 caps all for absurdity,
without even any of the redeeming qualities of the rest.   It
represents Bonaparte—facetiously described as the 'Exile
and the rock-limpet'—standing on the sea-shore at St. Helena
. . . the whole thing is so truly ludicrous,'' etc.[1]

---

[1] *Library Gazette*, May 14, 1842, p. 331.

OF JAMES A. McNEILL WHISTLER

Another writer says :

" This gentleman has on former occasions chosen to paint with cream, or chocolate, yolk of egg, or currant-jelly,— there he uses his whole array of kitchen-stuff. . . . We cannot fancy the state of eye which will permit any one cognizant of art to treat these rhapsodies as Lord Byron treated ' Christabel ;' neither can we believe in any future revolution which shall bring the world round to the opinion of the worshipper, if worshippers such frenzies still possess."[1]

In reply to these and similar criticisms Ruskin said :[2]

" There is nothing so high in art but that a scurrile jest can reach it ; and often the greater the work the easier it is to turn it into ridicule. To appreciate the science of Turner's color would require the study of a life, but to laugh at it requires little more than the knowledge that yolk of egg is yellow and spinach green,—a fund of critical information on which the remarks of most of our leading periodicals have been of late years exclusively based. We shall, however, in spite of the sulphur-and-treacle criticisms of our Scotch connoisseurs and the eggs and the spinach of our English ones, endeavor to test the works of this great colorist by a knowledge of nature somewhat more extensive than is to be gained by an acquaintance, however familiar, with the apothecary's shop or the dinner-table."

There is Ruskin in arms on the other side,—it making all the difference in the world which ox is gored.

---

[1] *Athenæum*, May 14, 1842, p. 433.

[2] See opening paragraph of Chapter II. of the first and second editions of the first volume of " Modern Painters."

RECOLLECTIONS AND IMPRESSIONS

What an interesting chapter in the history of appreciation it all makes. Here we have the critics fulminating against Turner in "egg and spinach" terms and Ruskin fulminating against the critics in "pot and kettle" terms. A few years later we have Ruskin fulminating against Whistler in the same old terms ; but Whistler greatly improved the language of vituperation by introducing humor, and answered with words that bit like acid and epigrams pointed like needles—the etcher in controversy.

"Produced as if by throwing handfuls of white and blue and red at the canvas," said the critic of Turner. "Flinging a pot of paint in the public's face," said Ruskin of Whistler. Beyond this, criticism begins to be personal.

And Whistler drew the line on the "pot and kettle" stage and brought suit for libel.

The case was heard in November, 1878, before Baron Huddleston and a special jury.

The cross-examination of Whistler by the attorney-general, who appeared for the defendant, was one of the features of the case, and brought out many of the artist's views concerning art and art critics.

It is said that during the trial one of Whistler's counsel was holding up the nocturne in controversy before the jury, when one of the counsel on the other side called out :

"You are holding that upside down."

"No, I'm not."

"I tell you, you are."

"How do you know which is the top and which is the bottom?"

"Oh, I don't know; only when I saw it hanging in the Grosvenor Gallery it was the other side up."

Whereupon—out of deference to precedent—the nocturne was reversed.

When Whistler was asked whether the nocturne represented a view of Cremorne, he answered:

"If it were called a view of Cremorne, it would certainly bring about nothing but disappointment on the part of the beholders. It is an artistic arrangement."

And again, when asked whether a certain nocturne in blue and silver was a "correct" representation of Battersea Bridge, he replied:

"I did not intend it to be a 'correct' portrait of the bridge. It is only a moonlight scene, and the pier in the centre of the picture may not be like the piers at Battersea Bridge as you know them in broad daylight. As to what the picture represents, that depends upon who looks at it. To some it may represent all that is intended; to others it may represent nothing."

"The prevailing color is blue?"

"Perhaps."

"Are these figures on the top of the bridge intended for people?"

"They are just what you like."

"Is that a barge beneath?"

"Yes. I am very much encouraged at your

perceiving that. My whole scheme was only to bring about a certain harmony of color."

Mr. Ruskin did not appear, but others testified in his behalf.

Edward Burne-Jones admitted the picture had fine color, but found absolutely no detail and composition. It was "bewildering in form," and "one of the thousand failures to paint night," and "not worth two hundred guineas."

All of which opinions have been reversed by time, —even to the value, which quintupled many years ago.

Mr. Frith—of whose art both Burne-Jones and Ruskin probably had opinions that could not be expressed in temperate language—presented his credentials as the author of the "Railway Station," "Derby Day," and the "Rakes Progress," and testified that Whistler's pictures were "not serious works of art." But, then, he confessed he had not been invited to exhibit at the Grosvenor Gallery, and, as every one knows, what is considered art in one exhibition may not be so considered in another.

And Tom Taylor, of the *Times*,—well, for Tom Taylor's testimony and opinions one must go to the "Gentle Art." It is his one sure niche in the temple of fame.

In addressing the jury, the attorney-general said "he did not know when so much amusement had been offered to the British public as by Mr. Whistler's pictures."

OF JAMES A. McNEILL WHISTLER

The verdict was for the plaintiff, and the damages assessed at one farthing ; which coin Whistler wore on his chain long afterwards.

The costs assessed against Ruskin amounted to £386 12s. 4d., and were paid by public subscription, one hundred and twenty persons contributing.

Concerning this suit, Ruskin said, " I am blamed by my prudent acquaintances for being too personal ; but, truly, I find vaguely objurgatory language generally a mere form of what Plato calls 'shadow-fighting.'" And long after, when a friend asked him about the case, he said, " I am afraid of a libel action if I open my mouth ; and if I can't say what I like about a person, I prefer to say nothing at all." [1]

Even Ruskin could not say what he liked about any one, though every one, including the victim, might like the manner of his saying it. Still, it will ever remain a matter of wonder how Whistler induced an English jury, who could not possibly understand him, to give him a nominal verdict and saddle the costs upon Ruskin, who was something of a popular idol.

Whistler's lawyers must have been cleverer than those of the other side. The attorney-general probably proved, as his speech indicates, a clumsy defender in a case involving nice questions of art.

Be it said to the credit of Whistler's sagacity, he always employed the best lawyers available. He

---

[1] John Ruskin, by Spielmann, p. 34.

147

once said, "Poor lawyers, like poor paintings, are
dear at any price."

While Whistler had practised the gentle art of
making enemies from the beginning of his career,
his suit against Ruskin was, so to speak, his first
public appearance, and he threw his dart at a shining
mark.

What his real feelings towards Ruskin were no
man can say,—for towards the public and his critics
he was one man, towards his art he was quite
another.

To the world he seemed the incarnation of vanity
and conceit ; to the few whose privilege it was to see
him at work he appeared, and was, the embodiment
of sincerity and earnestness, of simplicity to the
verge of diffidence.

It is impossible to conceive two personalities so different as Whistler at work and Whistler at play, and
all his controversies were play to him, the amusement of his hours of relaxation.

He sued Ruskin, not because his status before art
was in any wise affected, but because his status before the public was assailed ; not because he cared
the snap of his finger for any adverse opinion concerning his pictures, but because he felt that he had
a certain position, pose one might say, to maintain,
and because it amused him to sue one who was considered so infallible ; and he, no doubt, felt reason-

OF JAMES A. McNEILL WHISTLER

ably sure he would be more than recompensed by the solemn testimony of opposing witnesses.

Whistler has been so often charged with being a poser that in the eyes of the world he really must have seemed so.

He was a poser in the sense already indicated, —namely, he was one man before the public and another at work. In this sense every man clever enough to forget himself at times is something of a poser, for only the stupid who can talk nothing but "shop," wherever they are, are the same day in and day out.

Most men are able to leave their work behind and adopt a *rôle* more or less artificial in social intercourse. The brilliant few who make society possess this faculty in an eminent degree.

The objection that social England has against the shopkeeper is, no doubt, based upon many sad experiences that the shopkeeper brings his shop with him to dinner, and will not, or cannot, pose to the extent of forgetting his material concerns in the presence of the frivolous.

The preacher, the politician, the lawyer, the soldier may introduce a little "shop" in general conversation, for these occupations are supposed to have a more general interest ; but the butcher, the baker, and the candlestick-maker cannot. But preacher, politician, lawyer, and soldier make the better guests if they pose a little and forget, for the time being, their occupations.

149

RECOLLECTIONS AND IMPRESSIONS

Convictions must be introduced sparingly in social intercourse ; a very few go a great way.

Why not adopt and duly post some such salutary rule as this ?   In social intercourse the utterance of one's profound convictions shall bear the same ratio to one's total utterances on any given occasion that the speaker bears to the number present and participating in the conversation.   That is to say, if the conversation is between two alone, half that either says may be his convictions, the other half a polite, though futile, endeavor to understand the other's convictions.   If at a table of twelve, about a twelfth of one's real thoughts are permissible, and all that, in justice to others, should be attempted.

But, then, conversation is a lost art.   An Athenian could talk better about everything than a modern can talk about anything.   Cast a subject, a thought, so much as a suggestion, into a knot of Greeks, and in a trice, like dogs over a bone, they would be wrestling with it, and the less they knew about it the brighter the discussion.

Knowledge is the last refuge of the stupid.   Facts are the sinkers of talk.   Ideas are the flash-lights of the imagination ; and conversation depends not upon knowledge but upon ideas.   One who knows nothing of a subject may have more ideas concerning it than one who knows all about.   Women are frequently better conversers than men, because less hampered by facts.

Knowledge is a heavy weight for conversation to carry.   But of all the bores who find their way to the dinner-table the specialist in knowledge is the most hopeless. The man who knows everything about something is at the stupid end ; the man who knows something about everything at the brilliant, with a place at his right hand for the woman who knows nothing about anything.

Whistler was of the choice few who would never speak seriously of his serious pursuits in general conversation. At those very moments when he seemed to be saying most about art and artists he was in reality saying least of what he really thought. When he talked most of himself he said nothing that he really felt. It was almost impossible to draw from him a serious opinion concerning a picture or a painter. Though he might rail by the hour against this man or that, if the mood seized him, it all meant nothing.

In his studio, when at work, opinions and appreciations worth remembering would drop from his lips ; but he rarely committed himself ; not because his convictions were not clear, but because he seldom thought it worth while.

Once he was dining with quite a distinguished company. The conversation—possibly as tribute to the presence of so noted an artist—turned upon art, and finally upon a notorious picture, called " Nana," of a naked woman on a couch, that was quite a sensation in London. It has been seen on this side.

Loud were the expressions of approval. Whistler remained silent.

RECOLLECTIONS AND IMPRESSIONS

" What do you think of ' Nana,' Mr. Whistler ?" asked the distinguished lady at his right.

" Is it not wonderful ?—so life-like," exclaimed the distinguished lady at his left.

But Whistler, apparently spellbound by the bird before him, was silent.

" But, Mr. Whistler, you have not told us what *you* think about ' Nana,' " said the distinguished lady opposite.

At bay at last, he said :

" Really, madam, you know, it is quite—presumptious—quite, for one who—who is simply, as one might say, a painter, and therefore—you know—not entitled to opinions —to express himself in the presence of so—so many distinguished connoisseurs ; but—since you demand my opinion— as a highwayman would a purse—I yield to superior strength and say—with all deference—that ' Nana ' is—trash."

" Oh !"

" Oh, Mr. Whistler."

" But have you seen it ?"

" No."

" Then, how can you say it is trash ?"

" It must be—it—is so—popular."

" Will you go to see it ?"

" That is not necessary."

" But I want you to go with me to-morrow to see ' Nana.' " And the charming lady on his right insisted so imperiously that he should go with her and several of the company who wished to be of the party, that he yielded, saying, however :

" On one condition."

" What is it ?"

" That you will go with me afterward, to the National Gallery and see some pictures I am sure you have never seen."

" Some new ones ?"

" To you—yes."

It was agreed ; and the following day Whistler with several of the party paid each a shilling to see " Nana" stretched at

OF JAMES A. McNEILL WHISTLER

ease under a strong light at the far end of a dark room. It might have been a painting or "Nana" herself, the realism was so gross.

All save Whistler were in raptures over the wondrous thing. He was silent.

Then they went to the National Gallery, and he took them before one great portrait after another.

"But we have seen these before," chorused the voices.

"Impossible!" exclaimed Whistler.

"Oh, yes, many times," sang the voices.

"But you do not like them ; you detest them."

"Oh, no ! no ! no——— !"

"But they are not at all like 'Nana' ; they haven't 'Nana's' wonderful flesh-tones, 'Nana's' beautiful skin ; are not so life-like as 'Nana,' and beside 'Nana' you must consider them as poor, wretched daubs."

And so he took them from one masterpiece to another, repeating before each one their raptures over "Nana" until they were silent. Then he said :

"I have shown you some pictures that are considered good by those whose opinions are precious, and you have not found in one a single characteristic that you admired in 'Nana,' and you yourselves would not admit her to this glorious company ; therefore, again I say, 'Nana' is— trash."

In the sense, therefore, that he presented a careless, trivial, or cynical side to the public and a serious side to his art, Whistler was a poser, and during his idle hours he had the habit of amusing himself at the expense of any one who crossed his path. And why not? Did not the world try so hard to amuse itself at his expense? Were his feelings spared? Was aught of ridicule or insult that human ingenuity could devise withheld?

But his opponents were so clumsy that, save as he himself preserved their crude repartees, only his epigrammatic utterances are remembered ; and therefore he has all the blame for the controversies, while the truth is that, considering the flood of opprobrium poured out upon him in print and in speech, he said very little, took but occasional notice of his assailants. All he said fills but a portion of a small book,—the "Gentle Art,"—while his opponents have the balance ; and if all adverse personal comments of a despicable nature were gathered together from both sides of the Atlantic, they would make up many closely-printed volumes.

For a man who could write so well, Whistler exercised great restraint in writing so little, but—that little !

And yet it is a pity, from one point of view, that he wrote at all ; his art did not need it, and in the way of general estimation and recognition suffers not a little on account of it.

For twenty-odd years the public has been amused, startled, and irritated by the letters and utterances which make up " The Gentle Art of Making Enemies," and it will be many a long day before they are so far forgotten that Whistler's art will be judged wholly upon its merits.

If the " Gentle Art" did not exist as it does in its harmony in brown, English literature would lack a volume which is in itself a bit of art and unique of its kind. There is nothing at all like it, and only

OF JAMES A. McNEILL WHISTLER

Whistler could have done it. The book is a perfect expression of one side of his many-sided and extraordinary personality, and as such is therefore a work of art, and, at the same time, material which cannot be spared if the man is to be thoroughly understood ; but it reveals the side which is least worth understanding, it accentuates traits which are inconsequential, and it gives the public an entirely erroneous impression, because the public find it easy to buy and read the book, but difficult to so much as see the pictures, and quite impossible to understand them when they do see them.

In Whistler's life the writing of the few lines and the putting together of the matter contained in the "Gentle Art" occupied an almost infinitesimal fraction of his leisure hours, whereas for fifty years he painted, etched, and lithographed industriously ; yet, so far as the public of England and America is concerned, his controversies overshadow his art ; while to the French, who happily could not read the book, he is known only as an artist.

Criticism of art afforded Whistler a world of amusement, and the art critic was his especial aversion.

"That writers should destroy writings to the benefit of writing" seemed to him just, but that writers should criticise painting seemed to him altogether illogical.

And he quotes the critic of the *Times*, who said of Velasquez's "Las Menimas" that it was "slovenly in execution, poor in color,—being little but a combination of neutral grays and ugly in its forms."

And he shows how the same great critic praised a Turner that turned out to be no Turner. When this particular critic died, a few years ago, Whistler sorrowfully said, "I have hardly a warm personal enemy left."

And he showed how one said that Daubigny had neither drawing nor color, and another that the works of Corot to the first impression of an Englishman "are the sketches of an amateur," and another that everything Courbet touches "becomes unpleasant."

All these by the most eminent critics in the land, —men whose say-so in days gone by made and unmade, for the time being, the reputations of artists.

And he grouped together a number of Ruskin's dogmatic utterances, where in his enthusiasm for certain men he condemned others who were infinitely superior,—as, for instance, where he praises without limitations the work of the forgotten Prout, and says that Rembrandt's colors are wrong from beginning to end, and that "Vulgarity, dulness, or impiety will indeed always express themselves through art in brown and gray, as in Rembrandt;" and again where he places Rubens above Titian and Raphael, and compares an unknown Mulready with Albert Durer, to the disadvantage of the latter.

These things it pleased Whistler to do, and he has done them with rare piquancy in the "Gentle Art."

If what is contained therein savors in aught of malice, let it be remembered that public, critics,

painters were snapping at his heels during the years
that he was doing the very work which public, critics,
and painters now worship, and a lesser man would
have yielded to the storm of adverse opinion and
ridicule.

With the exception of a few friends and admirers,
he was absolutely without support during the period
when an artist most needs encouragement.

It is everlastingly to his credit that neither the
ridicule of others—"the voice of the nation"—nor
his own necessities, and they pressed heavily at
times, caused him to swerve a hair's breadth from
what he believed to be worth doing in art.

Nearly every great artist of whom we have any
record has at one time or another in his career
yielded to the temptation—frequently under pressure of dire necessity—to do something that would
sell. No such reproach can be laid at Whistler's
door.

The galled critics complained that he did not
treat them fairly,—that he selected small excerpts
from voluminous essays ; whereas, if he had reprinted the essays entire, language apparently plain
would have been reversed in meaning. For instance,
he of the *Times*, who had written of Velasquez,
complained that the quotation gave " exactly the
opposite impression to that which the article, taken
as a whole, conveys." It must have been an extraordinary article to transform what was quoted into
praise ; but Whistler, in reply, said :

RECOLLECTIONS AND IMPRESSIONS

"Why squabble over your little article? You *did* print what I quote, you know, Tom ; and it is surely unimportant what more you may have written of the Master. That you should have written anything at all is your crime."

Ruskin never complained of anything Whistler wrote. The one utterance which caused the suit for libel was probably the first and last that passed his lips. The eloquent old man never did pay very much attention to what others thought of him ; he was too busy with his own dreams and fancies.

He did write what Whistler quoted about Rembrandt, but the whole passage is a lament over the lack of appreciation of color, and is as follows :

"For instance : our reprobation of bright color is, I think, for the most part, mere affectation, and must soon be done away with. Vulgarity, dulness, or impiety will indeed always express themselves through art in brown and gray, as in Rembrandt, Caravaggio, and Salvator ; but we are not wholly vulgar, dull, or impious, nor, as moderns, are we necessarily obliged to continue so in any wise. Our greatest men, whether sad or gay, still delight, like the great men of all ages, in brilliant hues. The coloring of Scott and Byron is full and pure ; that of Keats and Tennyson rich even to excess. Our practical failures in coloring are merely the necessary consequences of our prolonged want of practice during the period of Renaissance affectation and ignorance ; and the only durable difference between old and modern coloring is the acceptance of certain hues by the modern, which please him by expressing that melancholy peculiar to his more reflective or sentimental character and the greater variety of them necessary to express his greater science." [1]

---

[1] Modern Painters, vol. iii., chap. xvii., paragraph 18.

OF JAMES A. McNEILL WHISTLER

Again, on the subject of color, he says :

" We find the greatest artists mainly divided into two groups,—those who paint principally with respect to local color, headed by Paul Veronese, Titian, and Turner, and those who paint principally with reference to light and shade irrespective of color, headed by Leonardo da Vinci, Rembrandt, and Raphael. The noblest members of each of these classes introduce the element proper to the other class, in a subordinate way. Paul Veronese introduces a subordinate light and shade, and Leonardo introduces a subordinate local color. The main difference is, that with Leonardo, Rembrandt, and Raphael vast masses of the picture are lost in comparatively colorless (dark, gray, or brown) shadow,— these painters *beginning* with the *lights* and going *down* to blackness ; but with Veronese, Titian, and Turner the whole picture is like the rose,—glowing with color in the shadows and rising into paler and more delicate hues, or masses of whiteness, in the lights,—they having *begun* with the *shadows* and gone up *to* whiteness.''

Ruskin said so much about art, and said it so dogmatically, that no one utterance gives an adequate conception of what he thought about any one man. Furthermore, while his language is crystal itself, his thoughts are often contradictory and confusing in the extreme.

For instance, no man with any sense of color whatsoever would group Leonardo, Rembrandt, and Raphael together as men who painted " irrespective of color,"—for no great Italian from the days of Giotto to those of Michael Angelo painted regardless of color ; on the contrary, color is the one conspicuous, brilliant, and beautiful feature of their work,

and the color-sense, as it existed in those days in all
its exquisite refinement, is, generally speaking, absolutely wanting in ours.

In all but color Rembrandt forgot more than most
of the Italians ever knew ; but in the use of color—
not imitatively, not after the manner of nature, but
decoratively and arbitrarily—the Italians forgot more
than Rembrandt ever knew ; and, so far as color is
concerned, there is absolutely nothing in common
between Rembrandt and Leonardo or Raphael,
while there is much in common between the two
latter.

It was not color, but *light*, that Ruskin appreciated, as is shown by a hundred passages, but by
none more *clearly* than that quoted wherein he says
of the three painters last named,—and the italics are
his,—"these painters *beginning* with *lights* and
going *down* to blackness ; but with Veronese, Titian,
and Turner the whole picture is like the rose,—
glowing with color in the shadows and rising into
paler and more delicate hues, or masses of whiteness, in the lights,—they having *begun* with the
shadows and gone up *to* whiteness."

When he held his exhibition in London, in 1892,
of "Nocturnes, Marines, and Chevalet Pieces,"—a
"small collection kindly *lent* their owners,"—he
once more printed in his dainty brown-paper-cov-
ered catalogue, beneath each picture, the early comments of press, critics, and people, and called it all
"The Voice of a People."

And what a collection of bizarre opinions it is, to be sure, from the serious *Times* to the lightsome *Merrie England*, which said :

"He paints in soot colors and mud colors, but, far from enjoying the primary hues, has little or no perception of secondary or tertiary color."

Which goes to show that the budding science of chromatics is not without effect on vocabularies.

Here we have the "kitchen stuff" criticism of Turner in 1842 paraphrased word for word in the mud and soot criticism of Whistler precisely fifty years later.

Is the jargon of criticism at once limited and exhausted? Are we to linger forever about the cook-stove in the depreciation of art? With the introduction of the steel range of mammoth proportions can we not find new terms of opprobrium? Besides, there are the gas and gasoline stoves of explosive habit, which ought to be suggestive of novelty in vituperation. But, alas, the critic is prone to repeat himself, and the language of the fathers is visited upon the children unto the third and fourth generations of them that hate.

And press, critics, and artists are convicted, once more, of incompetency. But what does it matter, save as a warning that will not be heeded? Are we any wiser in our generation? Were Whistler to appear to-day, as he did forty-odd years ago, would he be received with the praise his works command now? Hardly.

RECOLLECTIONS AND IMPRESSIONS

Many of his followers were quite as absurd in their misplaced admiration as the maligned public in its denunciation, and no one knew it better than he. He came upon two of them once as they were waxing eloquent before a sketch that had somehow escaped his studio,—possibly overlooked and left behind in some of his movings. He listened a moment to their raptures, fitted his monocle to his eye, took a look at this "masterpiece," and said :

"God bless me, I wonder where that came from. Not worth the canvas it's painted on."

And he turned away.

We who have been taught to see, not wholly but in part, may laugh at our betters who, when he first appeared, could see nothing at all ; but our virtue is acquired.

His attitude towards critics is summed up in the short but pointed article written in December, 1878, shortly after the Ruskin suit, and called "Art and Art Critics."

"Shall the painter, then (I foresee the question), decide upon painting ? Shall *he* be the critic and sole authority ? Aggressive as is this supposition, I fear that, in the length of time, his assertion alone has established what even the gentlemen of the quill accept as the canons of art and recognize as the masterpieces of work."

All of which is undeniably true. The painter must in the end judge of painting, and the sculptor judge of sculpture. But there are two distinct sides to a work of art,—to every work, for that matter: there is the relation between the worker and his work, and the relation between the completed work and the public,—the work being the intermediary between artist and people, his means of communication, his mode and manner of speech.

There is, therefore, the process of creation and the process of appreciation, of utterance and of understanding.

The painting of a picture is one thing, its appreciation by the public is quite another.

A man need not be a dramatist to watch the effect of a drama upon the audience ; a man need not own a vineyard to know good wine.

The critic stands, or, rather, should stand, between the public and the work he criticises, whether it be poem, painting, statue, or drama ; the mistake he commonly makes is in forcing himself between the worker and his work, and in trying to teach him something only another and better worker in the *same* art is competent to do.

Critics make most of their blunders in judging works according to preconceived notions as to how they should be done,—in condemning, for instance, a picture because not painted after prevailing modes and methods, because it is a departure, whereas with these considerations the lay-critic has nothing to do ; they fall entirely within the province of the painter-critic, the one man who is competent, in the long run, to pass upon the methods employed.

Every work is an appeal to the public,—its completion and exhibition make it such ; therefore, every work challenges the critical faculties, great or small, of those who see it. It is inevitable that some more interested should spring up to interpret, rightly or wrongly, the work to the public ; the artist seldom takes the trouble,—in fact, has neither the time nor the temperament ; his message is complete in the picture, others must understand it as best they can.

The playwright cannot address the audience save through the play, the poet speaks only through his poetry, the painter through his pictures, the sculptor through the forms of his creation. Seldom is an artist gifted with more than one tongue, and that tongue is his art. How, then, can artists interpret the work of artists ? How can the painter, who is dumb save with his brush, or the sculptor, who is mute save with his clay and chisel, tell the world anything about the work of others ?

It is the business of those who can speak and write to tell the people, not how the work was created, unless they were present, but how it impressed them as a finished thing. That is the province of legitimate criticism.

Every man who has done his best to understand, though at the risk of betraying his ignorance, has the right to say how he likes what he sees or hears or tastes. The opinions of some are worth more than those of others ; and these opinions, with the reasons therefor, we are delighted to hear. That is about all there is to sound criticism ; and in that sense comment and those whose profession is to comment are inevitable,—until the æsthetic millenium, when critics cease from troubling and the artists are at rest.

Ruskin, unfortunately, attempted the double duty of telling painters how to paint and the public what to like. With all his industry and considerable talent for drawing, he was not competent to tell painters how to paint,—though much that he said is accepted as sound,—and his judgments of the relative merits of painters and pictures were biassed by his own convictions regarding the way the work should be done.

His limitations were due to his strong preferences and violent prejudices. His devotion to Turner—a great painter—was one limitation ; lack of appreciation of Rembrandt was another ; failure to estimate Velasquez at his real worth was another ; and a lot of enthusiasms for men who are now forgotten are so many additional evidences of lack of judicial temper in Ruskin. But all these things are as nothings in comparison with the rich store of things said in English so strong, so simple, and yet so beautiful that it fairly intoxicates and rouses something akin to a religious enthusiasm.

A word concerning the "Voice of a People," as Whistler called his little collection of criticisms. What is it ?

In literature the "Voice of a People" makes itself heard at the bookseller's counter and over the desk of the circulating library,—and that, too, regardless of critics who praise this book and condemn that. Sometimes, before the Critic has spoken, the "Voice" is heard, and the presses groan with the burden of their task ; or, more often, after the Critic has had his say, the "Voice," disregarding labored precepts, calls loudly for what it is told it should not have ; and so in literature the "Voice" makes itself heard loud and clear and natural, and there is no mistaking it.

Likewise in the drama the insistent "Voice" demands trash or otherwise, quite regardless of the protest of the Critic. The run of a play is not determined by the criticisms. The opinion of the Critic is often foreseen and defied ; but neither writer, manager, nor actor can foretell the verdict of the "Voice,"—favorable often when least expected ; adverse often when least deserved.

But in art the "Voice"—stentorian in literature and the drama—sinks to a whisper so diffident that it cannot be heard amidst the trumpetings of the Critics.

The Critics—those whose business it was to write and talk about art—ridiculed Whistler, not the "Voice." Left wholly to itself, it is quite likely the "Voice" would have found much that it liked in the beautiful combinations of tones and colors, for there is nothing inherently repulsive in Whistler's work, as in much other that Critics command the "Voice" to praise ; on the contrary, his paintings are exceedingly restful to the eye, and exceedingly attractive as schemes of color if nothing else. The "Voice,"

OF JAMES A. McNEILL WHISTLER

left to itself, would say, " I do not understand them, but I like them,—just as I like music, without knowing much about it."

But the " Voice"—independent enough in literature, the drama, and even in music—dares not lisp in art until the Critic speaks. Then the " Voice" praises what he praises, condemns what he condemns, until the secret purchases and growing demand for the outcast confound both Critic and echoing "Voice." Then the "Voice" turns—as it has in the case of Whistler—and rends the Critics, unless those agile gentlemen change sides and praise what they formerly condemned.

Too bad that Whistler attributed the "Voice" of the Critic to that long-suffering animal—the Public, which, if often wrong, is always honest, and, in all but art—vociferous.

Concerning his habit of persistently impaling the critics, a writer says :[1]

" We wish that the catalogue did not, for the tenth time, contain quotations from all the dull things which bewildered criticism has said about him. Mr. Whistler is a wit, and should recollect that the same old joke must not be told too often to the same old audience."

But where is the joke ? In the criticisms or in their repetition ? If the criticisms were serious, then repetition is doubly serious.

---

[1] *Saturday Review*, March 26, 1892, p. 357.

RECOLLECTIONS AND IMPRESSIONS

Nor is it "the same old audience," but each year, each hour, a new audience. Of all the English-speaking people not one in a million have ever heard the joke ; and if joke there be, it is surely a gracious act to make it known.

The far-seeing publisher deftly detaches the favorable comment from uncongenial context and prints it boldly on the fly-leaf of the volume. Why should not author or painter print his page of deprecia- tions that, as Whistler says, "history may be cleanly written" ? And if preserved and printed once, why not for all time ?

The record of a people is not complete unless their likes and dislikes be known. What would we not give for the adverse criticisms of Shakespeare? And there must have been many besides poor Greene's. What would we not give for some of the off-hand comments of his fellow-actors and his fel- low-managers ?

The world conspires to deceive the world. The literature of adulation is carefully conserved until mortals, denuded of their frailties, become gods.

In the course of his career Whistler met with many bizarre appreciations, but none more astonish- ing than this :[1]

"To understand Mr. Whistler you must understand his body. I do not mean that Mr. Whistler has suffered from bad health,—his health has always been excellent ; all great

---

[1] Moore, Modern Painting, p. 6.

artists have excellent health, but his constitution is more nervous than robust. He is even a strong man, but he is lacking in weight. Were he six inches taller and his bulk proportionally increased, his art would be different.''

The classification of the prize-ring into feather-, light-, middle-, and heavy-weights makes its appearance in art ; genius, like jockeys, must weigh-in and -out. By rights, therefore, Paganini should have played the bass-viol and Napoleon should have been a drummer-boy. The painter must measure his canvas by his belt, and bant the masterpiece into shape. The gymnasium is the true school of art, and the dumb-bell is mightier than the brush.

''For if Whistler had been six inches taller and his bulk proportionally increased, . . . instead of having painted a dozen portraits,—every one, even the ' Mother' and ' Miss Alexander,' which I personally take to be the two best, a little febrile in its extreme beauty, whilst some, masterpieces though they be, are clearly touched with weakness and marked with hysteria, —Mr. Whistler would have painted a hundred portraits as strong, as vigorous, as decisive, and as easily accomplished as any by Velasquez or Hals.''

This is the sort of comment that follows but never precedes acquaintance. After knowing a painter, it is easy to discover all his physical characteristics and idiosyncrasies in his work,—so easy, in fact, that many critics prefer to pass on books, plays, and pictures on their merits without knowing anything about the authors, the actors, or painters ; for in the end a work must stand or fall by itself.

RECOLLECTIONS AND IMPRESSIONS

From an examination of the "Hermes," can this critic give us the stature of Praxiteles? From the "Nike" in the Louvre can he describe the unknown master? What does the "Sistine Madonna" tell him of the weight of Raphael, or the "Lesson in Anatomy" of the "bulk" of Rembrandt?

A man's physical condition may be—frequently is—reflected in his work. If he is an invalid, what he does is apt to show it,—though Herbert Spencer is a case to the contrary; but his physique is another matter. Genius is not a matter of inches. The weight of the brain is not controlled by the size of the body; still more independent is the organization and development of the brain.

If a man have strength and health—and these the critic concedes to Whistler—his work may be the work of a giant.

One of the greatest and strongest of Germany's living artists is almost a dwarf; the most virile painter in America to-day is short and slight.

The same critic, referring to the letters in the "Gentle Art," says, "If Mr. Whistler had the bull-like health of Michael Angelo, Rubens, Hals, the letters would never have been written." But, as a matter of fact, Angelo was "a man of more than usually nervous temperament." As any one at all familiar with his career, his many controversies, his voluminous letters, well knows, "his temperament exposed him to sudden outbursts of scorn and anger which brought him now and then into violent collision with his neighbors." His habit of ridiculing and annoying his fellow-pupils invited the blow from Pietro Torrigiano which gave him his broken nose. He was a weakly child and suffered two illnesses in manhood, but by carefully refraining from all excesses he regained and preserved his health. " His countenance always showed a good and wholesome color. Of stature he is as follows : height middling, broad in the shoulders ; the rest of the body somewhat slender in proportion."

The foregoing scarcely bears out the sweeping generalization that "the greatest painters, I mean the very greatest,—Michael Angelo, Velasquez, and Rubens,—were gifted by nature with as full a measure of health as of genius. Their physical constitutions resembled more those of bulls than of men."

As for Velasquez, who can speak authoritatively for him ?

While the physical characteristics of geniuses are habitually exaggerated, and the weak, the nervous, the delicate are made well and strong and "like bulls" in the enthusiasm of appreciation or the exigencies of theory, it would not be difficult to point out in history, art, and literature innumerable instances of men whose achievements afford no indications whatsoever of their bodily make up,—in fact, it is common experience that neither poet nor painter ever corresponds with preconceived notions, and to meet the one or the other is to court disenchantment.

If Whistler had been six inches taller he would not have been Angelo, or Rembrandt, or Velasquez, but—in all probability—a soldier.

OF JAMES A. McNEILL WHISTLER

VII

Supreme as a Colorist—Color and Music—His Susceptibility to Color—Ruskin and Color—Art and Nature.

SUPREME as a colorist, Whistler achieved fame as an etcher long before the world acknowledged his greatness as a painter. Even now it is the fashion to exalt his etchings to the depreciation of his paintings,—to say that he was a great artist in the one medium but unsuccessful in the other.

The following is a fair illustration of this sort of comment :

"Cool-headed conservatism should clarify the halo which encircles Whistler's portraits. The periodic 'symphonies,' 'harmonies,' and 'arrangements,' in gray and green, green and rose, purple and gold, or brown and black, have, or had, novelty to recommend them,—more novelty, however, than psychology. Apart from one or two, they are little beyond essays in subdued *Japonisme* with subtle dashes of Velasquez. The portrait of his mother alone shows adequate depth, for the overlauded Carlyle is merely a male replica of the single canvas wherein the artist seemed to lose—and to find—himself. It is not in portraiture, but in etching and lithography, that Whistler has disclosed the validity of his talent." [1]

[1] *The Critic*, vol. xxxviii. p. 32, January, 1901.

RECOLLECTIONS AND IMPRESSIONS

To which may be added the following comments since his death from leading American papers :

"Whistler in earlier life was a real etcher, easily the first of the nineteenth century. The number of his plates of the best quality is comparatively small. He soon lost his power or the incentive to execute it. His hand degenerated, his work became trivial and insincere. As a painter none of his pictures will ever explain to posterity the reputation, or the apparent reputation, that he enjoyed during his lifetime."

"It is, however, as an etcher rather than as a painter that Whistler will be remembered."

"Thus, setting aside the portraits of his mother, of Thomas Carlyle, Lady Campbell, and Miss Alexander, and the startling 'Nocturne in Blue and Silver,' and the 'Arrangement in Black,' it might be possible to count upon the fingers of one hand the finest examples of his brush."

Many others of similar import might be gathered, but the foregoing suffice. In reading them it should not be forgotten that the etchings, which are now praised without reserve, passed through the same stages of depreciation through which the paintings are passing ; so that, guided by the parallel, it is reasonable to expect the complete acceptance of the latter as masterpieces in the near future.

Broadly speaking, the order of acceptance has been :

First. Etchings and lithographs.

Second. Portraits.

Third. Color harmonies,—such as many of his figure-pieces, marines, nocturnes, and pure color compositions generally, none of which is fully accepted, some of which are scarcely known, and

Blue and Silver; Blue Wave, Biarritz

OF JAMES A. McNEILL WHISTLER

all of which are misunderstood, in spite of his many
explicit words of explanation.

Such has been the order of general acceptance
of his work ; but the order of real merit is almost
precisely reversed.

Whistler stands supreme,—

First as a colorist.

Secondly as a painter of portraits.

Thirdly as an etcher and lithographer.

As an etcher comparisons are drawn between him
and Rembrandt.

As a painter of portraits comparisons are drawn
between him and Velasquez.

As a colorist he is beyond comparison save with
the masters of the far East.

In etching and lithography and the painting of
portraits he, at most, simply did as well or better
what others have done before ; but in the composition of harmonies of color to please the eye, as
harmonies of sound please the ear, he accomplished
results which are unique.

What he did with the needle is not so wholly and
absolutely unlike all that had been done before as
to render comparisons impossible ; whereas with the
brush in his domain of color Whistler stands alone.
His art was his own ; he painted like no other man
dead or living.

His etchings were so fine, so subtle, that the world
had difficulty in comprehending them ; but it did
learn to like them, and that, too, at a comparatively
early date.   But even now his pictures are fully

understood by no one ; and yet they have had a profounder influence upon the art of to-day than those of any other master.

He opened the door of the East to the painters of the West and showed them how they might paint after the manner of the best there is in the Oriental world, and not only retain, but accentuate their own individualities.

The secret of Whistler's art, as of all great art, is that it was the absolutely true and unaffected expression of his convictions and of his impressions of the life and world about him ; and his impressions and convictions in the domain of color, like those of Beethoven in the world of sound, were worth recording.

He is to color what Beethoven is to sound, and his distinguishing merit is that of all the men of his century or of many preceding centuries he was the only one to treat color as a composer of music treats sound,—as material for the arrangement of harmonies to please the eye as music pleases the ear.

When Burne-Jones, in the Ruskin suit, was asked if he saw any art quality in "The Falling Rocket," he apologetically said, "I must speak the truth, you know," and then testified : "It has fine color and atmosphere," but of detail and composition "absolutely none."

As if the shower of fire of a falling rocket against the blackness of night could have sharp detail and composition ; as if anything were possible beyond "fine color and atmosphere;" and color and atmosphere are all Whistler intended. "My whole scheme," he himself testified, "was only to bring about a certain harmony of color," and, according to the only decently qualified witness for the other side, he succeeded.

Even Frith, the painter of "Derby Day" and the "Rake's Progress," said, "There is a pretty color which pleases the eye, but there is nothing more."

Why should there be anything more, if to please the eye were the painter's sole intention? Is it not as legitimate to please the eye with compositions of color, otherwise meaningless, as it is to please the ear with compositions of sound?

Profoundly speaking, color has no other object than to please the eye. The story should be told, the moral pointed, in black and white. The use of color imitatively, or to accentuate the characterization, is as base as the use of sound imitatively.

Color is to the eye precisely what sound is to the ear, and the highest use to which either can be put is the production of pure, not to say abstract, harmonies for the satisfaction of its respective sense.

As long ago as 1868 Swinburne, in a pamphlet on the Royal Academy exhibition of that year, said:

"No task is harder than this translation from color into speech, when the speech must be so hoarse and feeble, when the color is so subtle and sublime. Music and verse might strike some string accordant in sound to such painting, but a version such as this is a psalm of Tate's to a psalm of

David's.   In all of the main strings touched are certain
varying chords of blue and white, not without interludes of
the bright and tender tones of floral purple or red.   They
all have immediate beauty, they all give the delight of
natural things ; they seem to have grown as a flower grows,
not in any forcing house of ingenious and laborious cunning.
This is, in my eyes, a special quality of Mr. Whistler's
genius ; a freshness and fulness of the loveliest life of
things, with a high, clear power upon them which seems to
educe a picture as the sun does a blossom or a fruit.''

In language too plain for the slightest misunderstanding he has himself told the world precisely
what he meant his pictures to be, but the world will
not take him at his word.

Nearly thirty years ago, when the people wondered
at his calling his works "symphonies," "arrangements," "harmonies," and "nocturnes," he wrote :

"The vast majority of English folk cannot and will not
consider a picture apart from any story which it may be
supposed to tell.

"My picture of a 'Harmony in Gray and Gold' is an
illustration of my meaning,—a snow-scene with a single
black figure and a lighted tavern.   I care nothing for the
past, present, or future of the black figure, placed there because the black was wanted at that spot.   All that I know is
that my combination of gray and gold is the basis of the
picture.   Now, this is precisely what my friends cannot
grasp.

"They say, 'Why not call it "Trotty Veck," and sell it for
a round harmony of golden guineas ?' naively acknowledging
that without baptism there is no . . . market !'' [1]

---

[1] Gentle Art, p. 126.

OF JAMES A. McNEILL WHISTLER

And farther on he said :

" As music is the poetry of sound, so is painting the poetry of sight, and the subject-matter has nothing to do with harmony of sound or color.

" The great musicians knew this. Beethoven and the rest wrote music,—simply music ; symphony in this key, concerto or sonata in that.

" On F or G they constructed celestial harmonies,—as harmonies,—combinations evolved from the chorus of F or G and their minor correlatives.

" This is pure music as distinguished from airs,—commonplace and vulgar in themselves, but interesting from their associations,—as, for instance, ' Yankee Doodle, or ' Partant pour la Syrie.'

" Art should be independent of all clap-trap, should stand alone, and appeal to the artistic sense of eye or ear, without confounding this with emotions entirely foreign to it, as devotion, pity, love, patriotism, and the like. All these have no kind of concern with it ; and that is why I insist on calling my works ' arrangements' and ' harmonies.' " [1]

And concerning the portrait of his mother, which nearly every one admires for the subject while few pause to consider the color, he wrote :

" Take the picture of my mother, exhibited at the Royal Academy as an ' Arrangement in Gray and Black.' Now, that is what it is. To me it is interesting as a picture of my mother ; but what can or ought the public to care about the identity of the portrait ?" [2]

Within these few lines are contained Whistler's whole philosophy of art, his convictions and his

[1] Gentle Art, pp. 127, 128.   [2] Ibid., p. 128.

179

intentions ; the words are so plain a child may read and comprehend their meaning, and yet people will not understand him.

Whistler's art was purely sensuous, as the finest music is sensuous. He had no interest whatsoever in the many problems of life and death, in the story of any person or the traditions of any place.

He had less interest in the associations connected with Old Battersea Bridge than the boatman lazily floating by ; but at certain hours and under certain conditions, at twilight or at dusk, or in the fog, it made a long, tremulous line which pleased him, and he painted it.

The fact that the Thames bounds English history was of no consequence to him ; but the muddy river between lines of buildings and wharves and shipping, and covered by boats and crossed by bridges, furnished him endless compositions in line and color.

The glory and the romance of Venice made no impression on his art ; but in out-of-the-way places, where others saw nothing, he found scenes which inspired his etchings.

As an etcher and a lithographer Whistler played with the mystery of line, as in painting he played with the mystery of color.

There is an art of pure line as there is an art of pure form and of pure color. It is just as possible to make a lot of meaningless lines which please the eye in their curves and endless variety as it is to please the eye with combinations of colors.

OF JAMES A. McNEILL WHISTLER

Decorative patterns and designs, aside from color, are simply line harmonies.

A child loves to make straight and round and curved lines upon slate or paper.

The eye follows lines with a delight akin to that taken in form and color.

When the Savoy Hotel was in process of construction, and the great steel beams thrust themselves upward towards the sky, and there was a lattice-work of girders and a veritable song of line, Whistler, seeing it one day from a neighboring window, exclaimed :

" Hurry ; where are my things ?   I must etch that now, for it will never again be so beautiful."

High buildings, mechanical processes, modern costumes had no terrors for him, simply because he had no sentiment concerning them ; if they furnished him beauties of line or color he cared not whether they were new or old.

Whistler's art was as devoid of sentiment as that of a Japanese.

To our Western notions the everlasting convention that serves for a face in Japanese art seems hopelessly monotonous.   To them our painstaking characterization of the features and peculiarities of each person is no art at all, but grotesque caricature ; it is the subordination of art which is of universal interest to the eccentricities of the individual which are of local interest.

In Whistler's art one must not look for any solution of the problems of life, for any sign of the emotions which control human conduct,—for love and hate and fear, for hope and ambition, for the tortures of jealousy or the bitterness of despair,— these are all absent; his art is pure and serene. His works are to painting what the "Ode to a Grecian Urn" or "A Midsummer Night's Dream" is to poetry, and hence in human interest they fall far short of the tragedies, the epics, the romances of literature and art, and they must not be judged by standards he did not seek to emulate. He could no more have painted a "Crucifixion" or a "Last Judgment" than he could have carved the "Moses" or written "Hamlet." In every sense, save that of abstract beauty of line and color, other painters have excelled Whistler, but as the master of pure line and color harmonies he is supreme.

Whistler's etchings and lithographs were simply compositions in line, delightful harmonies in black and white. It is too bad to preserve their names or identify them with any locality, for their exquisite art is better appreciated if no distracting considera- tion is aroused. But, oddly enough, he occasionally made concessions in the naming of these that he did not in the naming of his paintings.

Take, for instance, that charming lithograph, "Confidences in the Garden,"—two ladies walking in the corner of an old garden. The garden is in the rear of his Paris home on the Rue du Bac. The ladies are probably Mrs. Whistler and her sister. But what does it add to the print to call it "Confidences in the Garden"?   Nothing at all.   On the contrary, the title at once suggests a host of considerations which conflict with the abstract enjoyment of the composition.

That sort of a title is precisely what he condemns for his paintings.   It is, however, one of the very few instances where his titles suggest anything more than the obvious subject.   For the most part he was consistent in choosing names that do not distract.

Even the portraits he did not care to have known as "Portrait of Mr. A——," or "Portrait of Lady C——," thereby catering first to the vanity of a sitter, then to the idle curiosity of the multitude.   His portraits were compositions in line and color, and, as such, were artistic creations.   That they happened also to be portraits of certain individuals was a mere coincidence.   The portrait feature, upon which people lay so much stress, was of the least consequence to him ; and just because he did not permit the photographic element to move him, he secured results which are far beyond the art of the "portrait-painter."

The sense of color is so lost to painters, as well as to laymen, that to talk of color compositions as one speaks of sound compositions is to challenge doubt and occasion surprise.   And yet there is a music of color even as there is a music of sound, and there should be a delight in color composition even as there is a delight in sound composition ; and this delight should be something fundamentally distinct from any interest in the subject of the composition. The subject may be a man, or a woman, or a field, or a tree, or a wave, or a cloud, or just nothing at all —mere masses or streaks of color ; the perfection or the imperfection of the color arrangement remains the same.

That the color-sense is lost to laymen, critics, and painters is evidenced by the ridicule that for thirty years was heaped upon Whistler for calling his pictures "harmonies," "symphonies," "nocturnes," etc. ; for adopting the more or less abstract nomenclature of sound compositions—music—to describe color compositions.

One paper described them as " some figure pieces, which this artist exhibits as ' harmonies' in this, that, or the other, being, as they are, mere rubs-in of color, have no claims to be regarded as pictures." Another says, " A dark bluish surface, with dots on it, and the faintest adumbrations of shape under the darkness, is gravely called a ' Nocturne in Black and Gold.' " Again, "Two of Mr. Whistler's ' color-symphonies,' a ' Nocturne in Blue and Gold,' and a ' Nocturne in Black and Gold.' If he did not exhibit these as pictures under peculiar and, what seems to most people, pretentious titles they would be entitled to their due meed of admiration. But they only come one step nearer pictures than delicately graduated tints on a wall-paper do."

And so in endless iteration and reiteration.

It never occurred to either painters or critics to

judge the pictures as if they were in reality so many "delicately graduated tints on a wall-paper." The color-sense was deficient. The pictures were judged by their composition, their subjects,—or, rather, not appreciated at all, but condemned, on account of their titles, which expressed exactly what the painter desired to convey,—namely, his attempts to produce harmonies in color independently of subject.

So far from Whistler's titles being absurd, they were so many frank attempts to tell the public what the painter was really trying to do. He might have been more obscure, like many a composer of music, and simply said, "*Opus* I.," or "*Opus* XX.," and so on. He did call three of his early pictures "Symphony in White, No. I.," "Symphony in White, No. II.," and "Symphony in White, No. III. ;" but the first, a full-length figure, was also known as the "White Girl" of the "Salon des Refusés," 1863 ; the second, a three-quarter length of a young girl in white, standing by a mantel, as "The Little White Girl ;" while the third, with no other title, is of two girls in white.

But for the most part he chose to describe each particular work as an arrangement of blue and silver, or black and gray, or flesh-color and brown, according to the predominating tones of the composition, thereby aiding the eye of the observer.

There are beauties of form devoid of color ;
There are beauties of color devoid of form ;
There are beauties of form and color combined.

RECOLLECTIONS AND IMPRESSIONS

Of the foregoing the first is familiar in sculpture, and the third is familiar in painting, but the second is scarcely observed at all, though color without form is found wherever color is used decoratively.

The ordinary house-painter endeavors to secure agreeable effects by the mere arrangement of colors. The interior-decorator endeavors—for the most part with disastrous results—to secure agreeable effects by the mere distribution of color. In a crude way the house-painter, the sign-painter, the decorator, the dyer, the dress-maker, are all color-composers, their object being to produce harmonies in color quite irrespective of line and form. They know nothing about drawing, they know nothing about modelling, but they try to please the eye by color arrangements.

To rightly understand the color-sense let us briefly consider the matter from its scientific side.

The ear has a range of musical sounds of from sixteen and one-half air-vibrations per second—the note of the lowest pipe of the great organ—to four thousand seven hundred and fifty-two vibrations per second, the highest note of the piccolo of the orchestra,—a range of about eight octaves.

Below sixteen and one-half vibrations per second, and above four thousand seven hundred and fifty-two,—as high, in fact, as forty thousand,—sounds are audible, but not musical, being either too low and throbbing or two high and piercing to be agreeable.

OF JAMES A. McNEILL WHISTLER

In all countries this range of musical sounds is divided into octaves,—the octave of any given note having simply double the number of air-vibrations.

At the present time, in the Western world, each octave is divided, as every one knows, into twelve intervals, indicated on the piano by the seven white keys and the five black.

For instance, the middle C of the piano has two hundred and sixty-four vibrations per second, the C above has, of course, just double, or five hundred and twenty-eight vibrations per second. In the chromatic scale these two hundred and sixty-four vibrations, which make this octave, are divided into only twelve intervals, an average of twenty-two vibrations to the interval. In the octave above the average would be twice that, or forty-four, and so on doubling to the end.

There is a change in pitch with the addition of so much as a fraction of a vibration per second. As a matter of fact, musicians can detect the variation of pitch caused by the difference of half a vibration per second in the middle octaves ; the power to detect changes in pitch due to fractional changes in vibrations decreasing towards the bass and treble.

With this power of discriminating a thousand degrees of pitch in a single octave the Western world is content to arbitrarily and mechanically divide the octave into but twelve tones and semitones.

The Arabic octave contains twenty-four quarter-

tones, and Oriental nations generally take cogni-
zance of intervals so small they seem to us discords.

Helmholtz requested a distinguished musician to
investigate this matter in Cairo, and this is the
report :

> "This evening I have been listening attentively to the
> song on the minarets, to try to appreciate the quarter-tones,
> which I had not supposed to exist, as I had thought that the
> Arabs sang *out of tune*. But to-day as I was with the der-
> vishes I became certain that such quarter-tones existed, and
> for the following reasons : Many passages in litanies of this
> kind end with a tone which was at first the quarter-tone and
> ended in the pure tone. As the passage was frequently re-
> peated, I was able to observe this every time, and I found
> the intonation invariable." [1]

All of which goes to show how susceptible the
highly-trained ear is to fine gradations and combinations of sound and how easy it is to become accustomed to coarse intervals when the finer are no
longer used.

The various notes as sounded by a great variety
of musical instruments constitute the raw material
from which the composer and performer produce
melodies and harmonies absolutely unknown to
nature, and which—judged by the only possible
standard, their emotional and intellectual effects—
are incomparably finer than any sounds in nature,

---

[1] Helmholtz, Sensations of Tone, p. 265.

finer because a human utterance, the play of soul upon soul.

The eye has a range of color-notes from four hundred millions of millions of ether-vibrations per second, the rate of the deepest red of the spectrum, to seven hundred and fifty millions of millions, the rate of the violet rays. The following table of vibration rates of the colors of the spectrum shows the vibration intervals which divide the pronounced colors :[1]

Color-sensation.	Ether-vibrations per second.	
Deep red.	400 millions of millions.	
Red-orange.	437 "	"
Yellow-orange	457 "	"
Yellow.	509 "	"
Green	570 "	"
Blue-green	617 "	"
Blue-violet	696 "	"
Violet.	750 "	"

This color-scale, as produced by a great variety of agents,—such as colored lights, glass, stones, metals, fabrics, dyes, stains, pigments, etc.,—constitutes the raw material from which the color-composer, painter, and decorator produce melodies and harmonies absolutely unknown to nature, and, judged as musical sounds are judged, are incomparably finer than effects in nature, because essen-

[1] Fleming, Waves and Ripples in Water, Air, and Æther, p. 252.

tially human, because produced by man for their emotional and intellectual effect upon man.

Theoretically the variation of a single ether-vibration per second changes the shade of the color; but while the trained ear can detect the variation in pitch due to a half-vibration of air per second more or less, ether-vibrations are so incomparably more rapid that the best the trained eye can do is detect about one thousand different tints in the spectrum. In other words, there must be an increase or decrease of three hundred and fifty thousand millions of ether-vibrations before even the practised eye is consciously affected.

It is, however, altogether likely that while the eye is not consciously affected without these great variations in frequency, it is *unconsciously* affected, and susceptibility to and skill in handling color depend upon this unconscious susceptibility.

It is pretty well established that the range of color-vision cannot be materially extended below the red or above the violet by practice, but susceptibility to color variations and the ability to distinguish gradations of tone within the scale can be increased almost indefinitely.

Education of the color-sense is the development of this *unconscious* susceptibility,—of the *feeling* for, as distinguished from a knowledge of, color.

A man may *know* all about color and have no *feeling* for it. On the other hand, a man may be singularly susceptible to color-effects without being able to name correctly a dozen shades.

OF JAMES A. McNEILL WHISTLER

Nothing educates the color-sense so much as steady contemplation of color-harmonies in nature and art. But unless a man possesses an instinctive feeling for color he will never select the best examples; whereas if his eye is exceedingly susceptible he will intuitively cling to the best the world affords.

Whistler was gifted with susceptibility to color in an extraordinary degree. Where, by way of illustration, the untrained eye can distinguish one or two hundred shades of color in the spectrum and the highly-trained eye a thousand, Whistler could probably distingush two thousand, and possibly *feel* as many more.

In fact, so keen was his susceptibility to color that intervals—to use, very legitimately, the musical term—quite imperceptible to others affected him greatly.

The neck-tie of a sitter once caused him no end of trouble.

The suit the sitter was wearing was of a light-brown tone; the ulster was of a darker Scotch plaid,—all softened in tone by time and wear. In so many shades of brown it certainly seemed to the casual eye that the shade of the brown silk tie the sitter had on found a place. But, no; to Whistler it was a discordant note, though half hidden by the garments. All available ties were exhausted,—even those of friends and neighboring artists were levied upon.   Others could see nothing inharmonious in many of the ties that were tried ; but they made Whistler positively uncomfortable,—just as uncomfortable as the leader of an orchestra is when an instrument plays a discord ; and it was not until the "Bon Marché" had been ransacked—for, not ties, but simply fabrics in shades of brown—that a piece was found that would answer.

Then, mark you, the brown of the tie was by no means reproduced in the portrait, but the brown as modified by all the browns and notes of the entire costume, and as still further modified by all the browns and all the notes and shades and lights of the studio.

During this search for a note of brown—a search which seemed to the sitter, and even to artist friends, finical in the extreme—the great painter one afternoon justified himself by showing some little pastel sketches of a model with bits of transparent drapery floating about her.   The sketches were on coarse brown board, and about ten or twelve inches high by five or six wide, and there were just a few strokes of almost imperceptible color to indicate the flesh tones and the draperies, all so slight as to scarce attract notice ; and yet each of the filmy bits of drapery had been dyed by the painter with as much care to secure the desired notes as he would take in painting a portrait.

No one who has not seen him at work can form any adequate notion of his extreme susceptibility to infinitesimal variations of color ; it exceeded that of any painter of whom the Western world has sufficient record for comparison.

A Frenchman has said :

" Whistler's works are dreams of color. The gray of them is unique. It is made of white, blue, green, of all the tints. It is the tender gray of England's coasts, of the North Sea, and of the sky that in summer is above it ; the horizon gray where the pale blue of the sky and the pale green of the sea unite and form one.

" It is a subtle shade, in accord with the penumbras in which he delighted. He was the musician of the rainbow. No one understood as well as he the mysterious relations of painting and of music, the seven notes and the seven colors, and the way to play these with the sharps and flats of the prism. Even as a symphony is in D or a sonata is in A, his pictures were orchestrated according to a tone,—the ' Lady with the Iris,' for example, a mauve flower placed in the hand of the figure, as a note and signifying that the portrait was to be a colored polyphony of lilac and of violets.

" More precision is lent to this curious æsthetic by the titles that he gave to certain small canvases representing twilights of Venice and of London, which he entitled ' Nocturnes,' in a parallel with those of Chopin, but of a Chopin serene and who dreams instead of a Chopin ill and who weeps. There, as in portraits, the gray of England's coasts appears, but bluer. It has in portraits the tints of twilight in ashes. In all his works he reveals the land of his origin, the land that has produced Edgar Allan Poe."

Many stories are told illustrating his susceptibility to color. Some of them are pointless ; but the fact they are told at all shows how this trait impressed both the artists and the public.

" One morning he had an engagement at a banker's, where he was to receive a large sum of money for a set of etchings, a sum that he happened to need very much at that time. He was busy chatting and showing some of his things to an appreciative visitor, who happened to know the circumstances, and considerately reminded him that he had far to go and that the American would probably be in a hurry and would not wait.

" ' Yes,' said Whistler ; ' but just look at this now,' pulling forward another canvas.   And so it went on, until his friend said : ' Whistler, you really must go !   That man will never wait for you.'

" ' What a nuisance you are !' he exclaimed ; but he got ready, and they started.

" They were tearing down the street at a great rate, when Whistler suddenly stopped the cab and made the driver go back to a certain spot,—and they had to go backwards and forwards for quite a while before they found the exact place, —in order to get a view of a certain little green-grocer's shop, with his fruit and vegetables outside, striped awnings, etc.

" Whistler put up his hands for a frame, squinted and twisted.   ' Beautiful !' he exclaimed.   ' Lovely ! I'm going to do that ; but I think I'll have him move the oranges over to the right more, and that green, now—let me see——'

" ' Whistler !' cried his friend, ' *do* come along !   That man will be home in New York before we get there !'

" ' What a nuisance you are !' declared Whistler, and was sulky the rest of the way.

" It was not a pose.   The painter was so enchanted by what he saw that banker and money were nothing to him at that moment.''

And it is said a visitor once found him at work in his studio.

" The furniture was of a pale gray ; the hangings were of the same color ; the window shades were of gray ; the model a woman with gray eyes, wearing a gray costume ; and the costume of the painter was also of the same prevailing color.

"Whistler refused to talk with his visitor until he had removed his flaming red cravat ; and, after a few minutes' conversation, commented upon the fact that the tone values of his coat and trousers were out of harmony."

An exaggeration, but it all might have occurred ; for has he not himself described, in "Gentle Art," how the loud dress of a critic destroyed his exhibition. "To have seen him, O, my wise Atlas, was my privilege and my misery,—for he stood under one of my own 'harmonies,' already with difficulty gasping its gentle breath, himself an amazing 'arrangement' in strong mustard-and-cress, with bird's-eye belcher of Reckitt's blue, and then and there destroyed absolutely, unintentionally, and once for all, my year's work !"

The analogy between the musical scale and the color scale has been many times noted.

Helmholtz [1] draws the following analogy :

F ♯ . . . . End of the red.
G . . . . Red.
G ♯ . . . . Red.
A . . . . Red.
A ♯ . . . . Orange-red.
B . . . . Orange.

---

[1] Physiological Optics, p. 237.

```
c . . . . . . . . . . Yellow.
c ♯ . . . . . . . . Green.
d . . . . . . . . . Greenish-blue.
d ♯ . . . . . . . . Cyanogen-blue.
e . . . . . . . . . Indigo-blue.
f . . . . . . . . . Violet.
f ♯ . . . . . . . . Violet.
g . . . . . . . . . Ultra-violet.
g ♯ . . . . . . . . Ultra-violet.
a . . . . . . . . . Ultra-violet.
a ♯ . . . . . . . . Ultra-violet.
b . . . . . . . . . End of the solar spectrum.
```

There is, of course, this fundamental difference between the two senses : the action of air-waves upon the ear is mechanical, simply a succession of beats, while the action of ether-waves upon the retina is chemical in its character.

The true analogy lies in the simple fact that the ear is susceptible to certain sounds produced by air-waves of certain frequencies, while the eye is susceptible to certain colors produced by ether-waves of certain frequencies, and it is possible to mechanically combine in one case the sounds so as to produce harmonies that please the ear, and in the other case the colors so as to produce harmonies that please the eye ; and so far as pure sound and pure color is concerned, the harmonious compositions need have no relation, imitative or otherwise, to anything in nature.

The uneducated ear prefers melodies which are more or less suggestive of sounds heard in nature,—

more or less realistic imitations of songs of birds, rippling of waters, falling of rain, rustling of leaves, crashing of thunder, etc. ; or if familiar sounds are not imitated, the title of the composition must suggest some incident, place, or scene more or less familiar, so the deficient ear may be helped out by the imagination.

The highly-trained ear, on the other hand, delights in abstract compositions of sound, in harmonies which have no perceptible relation to any sound in nature, and which do not suggest any person, scene, or incident in literature or history.

The purer the taste in music the more abstract the compositions that satisfy.

So far as the appreciation of color harmonies is concerned, the taste of the Western world is like unto that of the uneducated ear in music.

We are not content with pure color compositions as we are with pure sound, but we demand either imitations of natural objects or representations of historical, literary, religious, or emotional subjects. We must have something besides pure line and color.

A musician may strike a succession of notes, or a chord, and we are pleased, the ear is satisfied ; but if the painter simply sweeps his brush several times across the canvas, we are not satisfied, though the combination of colors be something more beautiful and harmonious than anything ever seen.   It is not a "picture" to us ; it lacks the "subject" to which we are accustomed.

And yet there are in existence certain canvases

RECOLLECTIONS AND IMPRESSIONS

by Whistler which are little more than color-schemes, and which in color-effects are among the most beautiful things he ever painted ; and in all the galleries of Europe there is nothing to compare with them in pure joyousness of color.

As children and men we enjoy the color-effects of fireworks against the blackness of night, and we enjoy the darkness and the shadows about us, the sudden light upon expectant faces, the dark-moving figures in the intervals. All this is delight in color,— color without sentiment, color without story, color without other thought or reflection than pure sensuous enjoyment ; and we even feel the tawdry cheapness of the attempt when by set arrangement the features of some local or national celebrity are presented. But when an artist who sees such a night-scene and paints it in such manner that the color-scheme is preserved and its beauty enhanced in translation, we demand something more. We demand, as did Burne-Jones, " detail and composition,"—in short, we demand the features of our local celebrity.

Until we learn to love color, as we love music, for its own sake, there will never be any decorations of homes and public buildings that will be worth while.

In days long gone by, in Italy during the Renaissance and before, in Greece during the Golden Age, color was enjoyed for the sake of color, regardless of the dictates of nature. If an Italian felt like making a background of blue or gold, he did so ; if a Greek felt like painting and gilding his sculpture,

198

he did so, until the Parthenon and its contents must have been gorgeous with color, laid on, not after the precepts of nature, but for the most part arbitrarily, to please the eye.

All decoration begins with nature and ends in convention.

In this progress from birth in the imitation of natural forms and colors to death in the rigidity of a hard and lifeless convention there is a maturity wherein lines and contours and colors play with perfect freedom, original forms and models being absorbed in the finer creations of the imagination.

Ruskin habitually confused the use of *color* with the painting of *light ;* while in truth there is no necessary connection at all between colorists and *lightists*,—to coin a word that will very legitimately mark a distinction.

The painting of light is the distinguishing feature of nineteenth-century art, and Turner was the apostle crying in the wilderness of darkness ; he was the first to successfully attempt the realization of sunlight. He keyed his palette up with the sun as the objective point, while the Italians who had influenced him had keyed theirs up simply to produce color-effects. They decorated walls and altars and painted pictures—as a potter decorates his earthen bowl—to please the eye.

Although Ruskin habitually speaks of Turner as a colorist, and undoubtedly says a great many fine things concerning color, he did not care at all for color apart from the delineation of form. To him color was useful only as a mode of drawing; in itself it was as nothing at all.

Speaking of his so-called "truths" of color, he says :

"All truths of color sink at once into the second rank. He, therefore, who has neglected a truth of form for a truth of color has neglected a great truth for a less one.

"That color is indeed a most unimportant characteristic of objects will be farther evident on the slightest consideration. The color of plants is constantly changing with the season, and of everything with the quality of light falling on it ; but the nature and essence of the thing are independent of these changes. An oak is an oak, whether green with spring or red with winter ; a dahlia is a dahlia, whether it be yellow or crimson ; and if some monster-hunting botanist should ever frighten the flower blue, still it will be a dahlia ; but let one curve of the petals, one groove of the stamens, be wanting, and the flower ceases to be the same." [1]

"The most convincing proof of the unimportance of color lies in the accurate observation of the way in which any material object impresses itself on the mind. If we look at nature carefully we shall find that her colors are in a state of perpetual confusion and indistinctness, while her forms, as told by light and shade, are invariably clear, distinct, and speaking. The stones and gravel of the bank catch green reflections from the boughs above ; the bushes receive grays and yellows from the ground ; every hairbreadth of polished surface gives a little bit of the blue sky or the gold of the sun, like a star upon the local color ; this local color, changeful and uncertain in itself, is again disguised and modified by the hue of the light or quenched in the gray of the shadow ; and the confusion and blending of tint is altogether so great

---

[1] Modern Painters, vol. i., part ii., sec. i., chap. v., par. 3.

that were we left to find out what objects were by their colors only, we would scarcely in places distinguish the boughs of a tree from the air beyond them or the ground beneath them."

"We shall see hereafter, in considering ideas of beauty, that color, even as a source of pleasure, is feeble compared to form. But this we cannot insist upon at present,—we have only to do with simple truth ; and the observations we have made are sufficient to prove that the artist who sacrifices or forgets a truth of form in the pursuit of a truth of color sacrifices what is definite to what is uncertain and what is essential to what is accidental." [1]

"It is, indeed, by this that the works of Turner are peculiarly distinguished from those of all other colorists,—by the dazzling intensity, namely, of the light which he sheds through every hue, and which, far more than their brilliant color, is the real source of their overpowering effect upon the eye, an effect so *reasonably* made the subject of perpetual animadversion, as if the sun which they represent were a quiet, and subdued, and gentle, and manageable luminary, and never dazzled anybody, under any circumstances whatsoever. I am fond of standing by a bright Turner in the Academy, to listen to the unintentional compliments of the crowd,—' What a glaring thing !' ' I declare I can't look at it !' ' Don't it hurt your eyes ?'—expressed as if they were in the constant habit of looking the sun full in the face with the most perfect comfort and entire facility of vision. It is curious after hearing people malign some of Turner's noble passages of light to pass to some really ungrammatical and false pictures of the old masters in which we have color given *without* light." [2]

"What I am next about to say with respect to Turner's color I should wish to be received with caution, as it admits

---

1 Modern Painters, vol. i., part ii., sec. i., chap. v., par. 8, 9.
2 Ibid., sec. ii., chap. ii., par. 12.

RECOLLECTIONS AND IMPRESSIONS

of dispute. I think that the first approach to viciousness of color in any master is commonly indicated chiefly by a prevalence of purple and an absence of yellow. I think nature mixes yellow with almost every one of her hues, never, or very rarely, using red without it, but frequently using yellow with scarcely any red ; and I believe it will be in consequence found that her favorite opposition, that which generally characterizes and gives tone to her color, is yellow and black, passing, as it retires, into white and blue. It is beyond dispute that the great fundamental opposition of Rubens is yellow and black, and that on this, concentrated in one part of the picture and modified in various grays throughout, chiefly depend the tones of all his finest works. And in Titian, though there is a far greater tendency to the purple than in Rubens, I believe no red is ever mixed with the pure blue, or glazed over it, which has not in it a modifying quantity of yellow. At all events, I am nearly certain that whatever rich and pure purples are introduced locally by the great colorists nothing is so destructive of all fine color as the slightest tendency to purple in general tone ; and I am equally certain that Turner is distinguished from all the vicious colorists of the present day by the foundation of all his tones being black, yellow, and the intermediate grays, while the tendency of our common glare-seekers is invariably to pure, cold, impossible purples.''

'' Powerful and captivating and faithful as his color is, it is the least important of all his excellences, because it is the least important feature of nature. He paints in color, but he thinks in light and shade ; and, were it necessary, rather than lose one line of his forms or one ray of his sunshine, would, I apprehend, be content to paint in black and white to the end of his life.'' [1]

---

[1] Modern Painters, vol. i., part ii., sec. ii., chap. ii., par. 17, 20.

OF JAMES A. McNEILL WHISTLER

For practical purposes truths of form are more essential than 'truths' of color ; to mistake the size, shape, solidity, and texture of anything is far more disastrous than to mistake its color. The color-blind get on very well in the world, often without knowing their defect ; but a person who was form-blind would not get on at all.

The correct appreciation of form is of such vital importance that two senses are brought to bear,—the sense of touch—the parent sense—as well as the sense of sight ; and without the co-operation of the sense of touch, sight would be comparatively help-less in recognizing solidity, texture, contours, etc. In the appreciation of form touch gets on very well without sight, while sight could not get on at all without touch ; but, happily, a sense so precious is never completely lost.

Ruskin constantly uses the phrases, "truths of form," "truths of color," and it is apparent that by these phrases he really means fidelity to natural effects. With him a drawing, be it of a stone, a leaf, a tree, a mountain, is not *true* unless it corresponds to the thing in nature ; nor is a light or a shadow or a color *true* unless it corresponds to the effect in nature.

Now, so far as art is concerned, those so-called "truths" are of the least importance.

Suppose a musician were to talk of "truths of sound," meaning thereby the more or less faithful imitation of the songs of birds, the rippling of waters, the roll of thunder. Every one would know that his art was of the most primitive character.

"Truths of sound," in the sense that Ruskin speaks of "truths of form" and "truths of color," are not tolerated in music. To attain certain effects, dramatic in character, imitations of sounds in nature are sometimes introduced, but sparingly, and unless with great skill the effect is disagreeable to even the uneducated ear, and if pressed too far it becomes grotesque.

One art is like unto another, and what are really "truths" in one are "truths" in another. It is immaterial whether the sense of hearing, sight, or touch is appealed to ; it does not matter whether it is a composition of sound, of color, of line, or of form that is under consideration, the fundamental principles of the art are the same ; and one of the fundamental propositions is : imitation is fatal to pure art.

It is the business of art to improve on nature, to take the raw materials nature furnishes—her forces, her forms, her lines, her colors, her lights and shadows, her sounds, her odors, her flavors—and produce from them harmonious and agreeable effects unknown to nature.

Whistler has said :

" The imitator is a poor kind of creature. If the man who paints only the tree or flower or other surface he sees before him were an artist, the king of artists would be the photographer. It is for the artist to do something beyond this : in portrait-painting to put on canvas something more than the face the model wears for that one day,—to paint the man, in short, as well as his features ; in arrangement of colors to treat a flower as his key, not as his model."[1]

Art begins with "truths," in the Ruskin sense, and flowers in "harmonies," in the Whistler sense. It begins with the concrete, with imitation, with fidelity to natural effects, and it develops by a process of abstraction until it attains the chaste perfection of a Greek temple or a Beethoven symphony.

Nature is never left entirely behind, and some arts are more dependent upon her than others ; but, generally speaking, the more abstract the art the higher it is ; the purer and freer it is from imitation or suggestion of natural effects, the nobler its attainment. Because poetry and music are almost entirely independent of nature and natural effects, do they as arts, from one point of view, outrank sculpture and painting.

Ruskin, of course, was by no means blind to these considerations, and when he talked of "truths of form" and "truths of color" he did not mean literal imitation, but he did mean the fidelity of a draughtsman, of a man whose eye and mind were on the thing or effect before him ; and his great work is one long attempt to show that Turner in his brilliant and fanciful compositions was still clinging close to

---

[1] Gentle Art, p. 128.

nature, that he painted rocks and trees and clouds and sunlight as they really were, and more beautifully than any man before or since.

All of which goes to show that Turner was not a colorist in the sense Whistler was.

The one used color as a means, the other as an end. To the one color, like line, or like black and white, was incidental to his composition—the composition, the conception, the dream, the fancy,—in short, the subject, being all important. To the other harmonies in color was the end in view, almost to the exclusion in some of the nocturnes of line and of form.

To Ruskin, even more than with Turner, color was simply a means to an end,—the more perfect imitation of nature ; hence his utter lack of sympathy for Whistler's work.

To pure color arrangements Ruskin was blind. He demanded a relation and significance beyond the mere color harmony. Lines or waves of color placed side by side arbitrarily, and with no more relation to nature than so many notes of music, had no meaning for him, whereas for Whistler they meant practically all there is to the science and art of color.

To Ruskin the blue hair of a Greek statue would have seemed absurd and childish ; to the Greek it would have been simply a color-note in the place where it was needed to perfect the color-scheme.

So utterly wanting is the sense of color-music in the modern world that we like our sculpture in

either ghastly marble, or, still more perversely, with
the yellow hues and dirt and dinginess wrought by
time and the elements, whereas those who created
the greatest sculpture known subdued all garish
qualities by the use of gold and bronze and color,
not imitatively, but arbitrarily, to please a highly
cultivated fancy.

From descriptions of Ruskin's home, "Brant-
wood," it is clear that he had no craving for harmonious effects about him. Discords did not disturb
him ; he could return with no sensations of discom-
fort from the keen appreciation of natural beauties
to rooms which would be intolerable to any one
like Whistler with an instinct for proportion and
color.

The house had "a stucco classic portico in the
corner, painted and grained and heaped around
with lucky horseshoes, highly black-leaded." The
incongruity of the painting and graining—so contrary to all Ruskin's teachings—and black-leaded
horseshoes surprised even his friendly biographer.

His own room "he papered with naturalistic
fancies to his own taste," and on the walls were "a
Dürer engraving, some Prouts and Turners, a couple
of old Venetian heads, and Meissonier's 'Napoleon,'"—a typical collector's conglomeration.

The walls of the dining-room were painted "duck-
egg," whatever that color may be, and covered with
an even more heterogeneous collection of pictures,
—"the 'Doge of Gritta,' a bit saved from the great

RECOLLECTIONS AND IMPRESSIONS

Titian that was burnt in the fire at the Ducal Palace in 1574 ; a couple of Tintorets ; Turner and Reynolds, each painted by himself in youth ; Raphael, by a pupil, so it is said ; portraits of old Mr. and Mrs. Ruskin and little John and his ' boo hills.' "

His study was " papered with a pattern specially copied from Marco Marziali's 'Circumcision' in the National Gallery, and hung with Turners." There was a crimson arm-chair and a " polished-steel fender, very unartistic," his biographer remarks ; " red mahogany furniture, with startling shiny emerald leather chair-cushions ; red carpet and green curtains." This is the sort of room wherein Ruskin worked and wrote. It simply illustrates the truth that it is one thing to write and talk about color and a far different thing to really *feel* color.

It is the custom to call every man who paints in high key or uses brilliant colors a colorist, as Ruskin called Turner and Rubens colorists ; but it is not the mere use of color that makes a man a colorist, but the use he makes of it, the object he has in mind in using it.

The mechanical draughtsman and the architect may use on their plans and designs all the known colors, but no one would think of calling either a colorist.

In painting still-life a man may exhaust the palette and yet be no colorist. In painting portraits one man may require his sitters to dress in bright colors, another in sober blacks, grays, or browns, with the result that one set of portraits fairly dazzle the beholder, while the other scarce attracts attention ; and yet the former may not be the work of a colorist while the latter may.

The determining factor is the attitude of the painter towards color. If he uses color imitatively, or as incidental to drawing, or as a means to some end other than the production of color harmonies, he is not a colorist ; but if his delight is in color, if he uses color for the sake of color, for the sake of charming the eye, as the ear is charmed by music, then he is a colorist.

No hard and fast line of demarcation can be drawn, since every painter is something of a colorist ; but between the two extremes of the painter on one hand who uses color imitatively or as incidental to drawing and the colorist who produces and delights in pure color schemes and harmonies there is a wide interval.

Whistler, in his love of color, approached the latter extreme ; but it was only when he practised decoration that he could indulge his fancy without limitations. When he brought the Leyland dining-room into harmony with his " Princess of the Land of Porcelain" by the use of blue and gold, line and form—though somewhat apparent—were virtually negligible quantities ; and when he arranged the reception-room of the house in Rue du Bac, and his own studio, the only considerations were the color-effects.

RECOLLECTIONS AND IMPRESSIONS

In his "White Girl" of 1863 Whistler began in a large way his symphonies in color ; and while in pictures like the "Thames in Ice," "The Music Room," and "At the Piano" he painted along more conventional lines, these departures were infrequent and in themselves exhibited his predilection for color. It was simply impossible for him to paint any picture without making the color harmony a prime object.

Not long after the "White Girl," which was "Symphony in White, No. I.," followed the other experiments in white, known as Symphonies Nos. II. and III.

Then came—the chronological order is not important—the Japanese group, "The Princess of the Land of Porcelain," "The Gold Screen," "The Balcony," the "Lange Leizen," and others, in which the figures and accessories, though still prominent, were made subordinate to the brilliant color schemes. The compositions were still obvious, but the color incomparably more so.

Then the "Nocturnes," in which detail and composition were refined away, and little remained but color-effects so exquisite that they seemed, and still seem, beyond the power of brush, and more like some thin glazes and enamels than paintings on canvas.

As music in color the "Nocturnes" and certain of the "Harmonies" and "Symphonies," wherein detail is as nothing and the color everything, are Whistler's most exquisite—the word is used advisedly—achievements. Others will equal his portraits before they equal his "Nocturnes."

As a still further step towards pure color composition he had in mind for years a series of pictures, pure creations of fancy, somewhat suggestive of the Japanese group, but less realistic—just color-music. Happily, the sketches are in existence, and afford some indication of the color-dreams that floated through the great painter's imagination. They show how musical color is when freed from entangling associations and used broadly and decoratively.

We have, then, the following phases, rather than "periods," in his mastery of color :

1. That wherein composition and detail predominate, though color is the motive.

2. That wherein composition and detail are still conspicuous, but are subordinate to the color scheme.

3. That wherein composition and detail are practically lost in the effort to produce subtle color harmonies.

4. That wherein the sole object is color-music, quite regardless of other considerations.

This progress from the, so to speak, tentative use of color in connection with more or less conventional composition to the triumph of color and suppression of composition is abundantly illustrated in his works. It would not be difficult to arrange an exhibition of four groups of about three canvases each, which would illustrate each phase. Such an exhibition would do more to enlighten the public regarding his work than any number of exhibitions of a large number of pictures gathered and grouped in the usual way.

Regarding the use of flat tones he is reported to have once said :

"House-painters have the right idea about painting, God bless them."

How far removed from Ruskin, who said :

" Hence, wherever in a painting we have unvaried color extended even over a small space, there is falsehood.   Nothing can be natural which is monotonous ; nothing true which only tells one story."

To Ruskin nature was all in all ; to Whistler color was of first consideration.   The one looked at color to find natural effects ; the other looked at nature to find color-effects.

Whistler chose intuitively those scenes and those hours of the day when he would be least hampered by rigid requirements of line and form.

He frequently painted the sea under strong light ; but under any light water presents itself in broken lines and large masses.

He was a master of line in the high sense that with a few lines he could render not only the character but the characteristics of whatever was before him.   He was a master of form,—even as Ruskin uses the term,—since he could, when the conditions required it, express the most subtle contours in terms of light and shade and color ; but he cared less for the bald realities of sunlight than for the shadows of dusk and the mysteries of night.

He has himself said:

" The sun blares, the wind blows from the east, the sky is bereft of cloud, and without all is of iron. The windows of the Crystal Palace are seen from all points of London. The holiday-maker rejoices in the glorious day, and the painter turns aside to shut his eyes.

" How little this is understood, and how dutifully the casual in nature is accepted as sublime, may be gathered from the unlimited admiration daily produced by a very foolish sunset.

" The dignity of the snow-capped mountain is lost in distinctness, but the joy of the tourist is to recognize the traveller on the top. The desire to see for the sake of seeing is, with the mass, alone the one to be gratified, hence the delight in detail.

" And when the evening mist clothes the riverside with poetry, as with a veil, and the poor buildings lose themselves in the dim sky, and the tall chimneys become campanili, and the warehouses are palaces in the night, and the whole city hangs in the heavens, and fairy-land is before us,—then the wayfarer hastens home ; the working-man and the cultured one, the wise man and the one of pleasure cease to understand, as they have ceased to see ; and Nature, who, for once, has sung in tune, sings her exquisite song to the artist alone, her son and her master,—her son in that he loves her, her master in that he knows her."[1]

And it was his habit to paint when the studio was filled with gloom and lengthening shadows crept across the floor ; when it was so dark the dull eye

---

[1] Gentle Art, pp. 143, 144.

of sitter or chance visitor could scarce distinguish the figure on the canvas.

This "painting in the dark," as some have called it, was a singular trait. He would paint with increasing force and effect as the room became darker and darker, until it seemed as if the falling of night was an inspiration.

Once a sitter asked him how it was possible to paint when it was so dark.

"As the light fades and the shadows deepen all petty and exacting details vanish, everything trivial disappears, and I see things as they are in great strong masses : the buttons are lost, but the garment remains ; the garment is lost, but the sitter remains ; the sitter is lost, but the shadow remains ; the shadow is lost, but the picture remains. And *that* night cannot efface from the painter's imagination."

People never could understand his attitude towards nature. When he spoke of the "unlimited admiration daily produced by a very foolish sunset," and how "the dignity of the snow-capped mountain is lost in distinctness, but the joy of the tourist is to recognize the traveller on the top," he at once puzzled and irritated the lay mind, for is not the sunset beautiful? and the traveller on the highest peak of greater interest than the mountain?

When a lady one day rushed up to him and enthusiastically exclaimed :

"Oh, Mr. Whistler, I have just been up the river, and it reminded me so much of your pictures."

And he replied :

"Indeed ! Then, Nature is looking up,"—people resented it as vanity.

But it was not vanity. It was simply his attitude towards nature and art.

If some one had said to Mendelssohn, "I have just been in the woods and heard sounds that were just like some of your "Songs without Words," Mendelssohn would have been surprised, and might well have replied, "Then, the birds are doing better."

Concerning nature, Whistler said :

"That nature is always right is an assertion artistically as untrue as it is one whose truth is universally taken for granted. Nature is very rarely right ; to such an extent, even, that it might almost be said that nature is usually wrong. That is to say, the condition of things that shall bring about the perfection of harmony worthy a picture is rare, and not common at all.

"This would seem, to even the most intelligent, a doctrine almost blasphemous. So incorporated with our education has the supposed aphorism become, that its belief is held to be part of our moral being ; and the words themselves have, in our ear, the ring of religion. Still, seldom does nature succeed in producing a picture." [1]

One should never confound art with nature ; they are antithetical terms. There is no art in nature ; there should be no nature in art. And what is art is not nature, and what is nature is not art.

Nature is the raw material, art is the finished product ; and art should no more resemble nature

---

[1] Gentle Art, p. 143.

than a house resembles a cave. And to the extent that art slavishly imitates nature is it of the cave-dwelling variety.

There is no color that is not found in nature. There is no combination of colors a hint of which cannot be found in nature. But it is the business of art to take the colors, accept the hints, and produce combinations and effects not found in nature.

It is not the business of the artist to paint anything as it is, but everything as *he* sees it.

Yet the public demand that a tree shall be reproduced as *they* see it,—that the picture shall be a substitute for the reality. Why not go to the window and look at the tree? For, as a *tree*, with its quivering leaves and the infinite play of light and shadow, it is more beautiful than any realistic photograph, drawing, or painting possibly could be. But to see the reflection of the tree in the depths of a human soul one must turn to art, to poetry, to music, or to painting. The reflection may not at all resemble the reality any more than Keats's "Ode to a Nightingale" resembles the bird or the song of the bird ; but it will be far more interesting and far more beautiful because a human expression.

The child's mud-house and the boy's snow-man are of greater concern to humankind than all the plains and mountains of the earth.

VIII

The Royal Society of British Artists—In Paris once more—At Home and at Work.

In June, 1886, Whistler was elected president of the Royal Society of British Artists.

Prior to that time he had exhibited in the rooms of the society in Suffolk Street, and he was no doubt elected to give life to a moribund association. He succeeded beyond the wildest anticipations of the most sanguine members.

He rearranged the exhibitions by excluding sufficient of the unworthy to leave ample space on the walls for the proper exhibition of such pictures as were accepted.

When the Prince of Wales, now King Edward, visited the galleries for the first time, Whistler, as president, received him. And when the prince said he had never before heard of the society and asked its history, Whistler, with the grace of a courtier, replied :

" It has none, your Highness. Its history dates from to-day."

Two years of so revolutionary a president were all the ancient association could stand. As has been well said :[1]

---

[1] London *Times*, July 18, 1903.

RECOLLECTIONS AND IMPRESSIONS

" That Suffolk-Street episode was, perhaps, the oddest of an odd career. The most mediocre and middle-class of all the artistic societies of London was in low water, and the thought occurred to some revolutionary members to make Whistler president. It was like electing a sparrow-hawk to rule a community of bats. Some of the bats moved out, some followers of the sparrow-hawk came in ; but the interesting new community did not last long. The suburban ladies, who had been the support of the Society of British Artists, were shocked at the changes. They found no pleasure in the awning stretched across the middle of the room, the battened walls, the spaced-out 'impressionist' pictures, and the total absence of the anecdotes and bright colors which they loved. A few hundred visitors of another sort came, and were charmed, but the commercial test of success was not satisfied. Before long Whistler ceased to be president, and the society, under a more congruous chief, ' relapsed to its ancient mood.' "

When he failed of re-election many of his friends resigned.

" It is all very simple," he said. " The ' Royal Society of British Artists' has disintegrated,—the ' Artists' have come out, the ' British' remain."

When interviewed to obtain his explanation of the "state of affairs :"

" The state of affairs ?" said Mr. Whistler, in his light and airy way, raising his eyebrows and twinkling his eyes, as if it were all the best possible fun in the world ; " why, my dear sir, there's positively *no* state of affairs at all. Contrary to public declaration, there's actually nothing chaotic in the whole business. On the contrary, everything is in order, and just as it should be,—the survival of the fittest as regards the presidency, don't you see ; and, well—Suffolk Street is itself again ! A new government has come in ; and, as I told the members the other night, I congratulate the society on the result of their vote : for no longer can it be said that the right man is in the wrong place. No doubt their pristine sense of undisturbed somnolence will again settle upon them after the exasperated mental condition arising from the un-natural strain recently put upon the old ship. Eh? what? ha ! ha !''

He painted a signboard for the entrance to the galleries,—a lion and a butterfly,—a " harmony in gold and red," with which, he says, " I took as much trouble as I did with the best picture I ever painted."

But his successor in office clothed the golden lion " with a coat of dirty black," and effaced the butter-fly entirely ; whereupon he called the society to task for destroying the work of a fellow-artist, and the entire episode appears in the " Gentle Art" as only he could tell it.

In 1887 he married the widow of E. W. Godwin, the architect of the " White House," and not long after they went to live in Paris, at 110 Rue du Bac.

The narrow passage-way that leads from the street to where they lived is, like thousands of others in Old Paris, just an archway between two shops, un-promising and uninviting.

Passing through, one finds a small paved court immediately in the rear, and on three sides of this court the entrances and windows of the apartments and houses opening therefrom.

The court itself is not without interest. On one

side there is an old bronze fountain, long since dry ; about the walls a sculptured frieze, much the worse for wear ; everything of by-gone days,—the very architecture, in all its details, of another generation.

Whistler's entrance was on the ground floor, just across the little court. On a memorable day the bell was answered by a solemn-faced English servant,—possibly more than ordinarily solemn-faced, because that particular morning he was in great disfavor, and was subsequently discharged for a cumulation of shortcomings which would have exhausted the patience of an ordinary man thrice over. But Whistler—all impressions to the contrary, notwithstanding—was a man of infinite patience with sitter and servant,—the work of the latter being considerably lighter than that of the former. Under only the greatest provocation would he discharge either.

Passing through the door, one went down several steps into the small hall, and through that into the reception-room.

This room was a revelation of the personality of the artist,—simple, dignified, harmonious ; it was restful and charming to the last degree. The details were so unobtrusive that it is difficult to recall particular features. The floor was covered with a coarse, dark-blue matting ; the panelled walls were in pure white and blue, while the ceiling was in a light shade of blue. The room stood firmly on its feet, unlike so many in even the best of houses, which have floors so light and walls so dark that everything is topsy-turvy.

Color seeks and finds its level; light floors, with darker walls and ceilings, reverse the natural order of things, and compel people to live on their heads.

The few pieces of furniture were of an old pattern, graceful almost to fragility, and covered with some light stuff which harmonized with the tone of the walls.

There were but two pictures in the room, one at each end, both sketches by Whistler, "harmonies" or "arrangements" in color rather than compositions. The "key" being blue, the pictures blended with the walls, as all pictures should, as if part of the original scheme of decoration.

When a visitor, who was fascinated by the color of these two studies, asked the painter if he would part with them, he said :

"God bless me, no! I am going to do something big some day from those. Pretty, eh?"

His studio was filled with just such "notes" and "jottings" of schemes in color and composition, and from each it was his intention to work out something more important and complete ; but such was the fertility of his imagination that no man could hope to carry even a fraction to finished conclusions.

Near the fireplace, at one end of the room, was a little old-fashioned table covered with writing-materials,—paper of the smallest size, a dainty inkstand, and several quill pens. This was the table of controversy, the battlefield of disputation, the veritable mount of irony, while the ink-well was the fountain of exquisite sarcasm, and the quill pens the scalpels which laid bare the vital recesses of unlucky opponents.

It was the habit of the painter, in his idle moments, to sit at this little table, with a small cup of coffee and a cigarette, and write those barbed and pointed notes which, like so many banderillas, irritated to frenzy the bulls they were aimed at.

The far side of the room opened into one of those quaint old gardens so often found tucked away in the midst of crumbling buildings on the ancient thoroughfares. Its narrow confines were enlarged to the eye by winding, gravelled walks and vistas of flowers and bushes ; the rickety seats, half hidden by the foliage, invited the loiterer to repose, and the high wall beyond suggested the gloomy confines of some convent or deserted monastery.

"A picturesque spot. Once at dusk there came the tinkle of a far-off bell, as if for vesper prayers ; the years rolled back, and visions of other days flitted along the garden paths ; stately dames in rich brocades, with powder, patch, and high coiffure, and gallant courtiers with graved and jewelled blades, whose whispered vows were no more stable than the sound of rustling leaves."

Here of a Sunday afternoon Mrs. Whistler frequently served tea, and in this garden he made some of his best lithographs.

At home Whistler was the most delightful of— guests. The cares of hospitality sat lightly upon him.

OF JAMES A. McNEILL WHISTLER

To the caller who had come at the appointed hour, and had waited for thirty or forty minutes, he would apologize so delightfully for the "unpardonable delay," that a prince could take no offence, much less an ordinary visitor, who could profitably spend the time in studying the harmonious surroundings.

It is difficult to describe the charm of his manner, so different from the notion of it that prevails generally.

He was far more easy of approach than most celebrities ; and once within the charmed circle, he was the most agreeable and companionable of living men.

He would make the diffident feel instantly at ease, and he would exert himself to interest even the stupid visitor, but he would not encourage him to come again.

His own talk was so bright that it was unnecessary for any guest to say much,—a capacity for listening appreciatively being the best qualification. Still, he did not monopolize the conversation. He himself was one of the keenest listeners that ever sat at a dinner-table ; nothing escaped him. And if by chance some one said a good thing, he was the first to applaud it.

In company it was impossible to draw him into serious discussion. If the attempt were made, it usually led to a monologue on his part on some branch of the topic under discussion,—a monologue so extravagant, so funny, so irresistible in its humor and denunciation that the entire company would turn and listen with delight.

No one who has ever heard his comparison of the Englishman who carries his tub and sponge on the top of the coach to parade his cleanliness with the French who had vast public baths before England was discovered can ever forget the inimitable wit and humor and—underlying truth of it all. Again, his description of the Germans,—a people that call a glove a hand-shoe. Well, it is idle to even call to mind these things ; they will never be heard again, and no report could do them justice.

A lady, after visiting him, said, " He is like no other human being ; a creature of moods and epigrams, but perfectly delightful. I feel as if I'd been conversing with a flash of lightning in a brown velvet coat."

No man could draw him out of malice aforethought. It was fatal to say :

" Mr. Whistler, do tell that story of the——"
etc.

Of that sort he was no story-teller at all, and if persistently urged, would close up like a clam ; but, if left to himself, he would take part in any conversation that might be started, and would soon take the lead, not obviously or offensively, but naturally, and say things that would make the professed wit dumb with envy. He would say things he had said, or even printed, before, if the subject warranted it. He might even go a bit out of his way to drag in a good thing which he thought would fit ; but for the most part his talk was the spontaneous utterance of the occasion.

He was known to every "chef" and "mâitre d'hôtel" in London and Paris,—for, while he ate and drank most sparingly, he was exceedingly fastidious.

He did not care greatly for the large caravansaries like the "Ritz," where people go to perform in public astounding gastronomic feats ; but he knew every place in Paris where a really good dish was to be had at a moderate price, and every such place gave him the best it had.

Nearly every sketch, drawing, or portrait of Whistler gives some phase of his many-sided personality, but not one—not even those by himself—gives anything like an adequate conception.

He was a man most difficult to place on canvas. He could not be grasped and held long enough. He himself tried it, but with only moderate success. Others have tried it and failed completely,—that is, failed to portray him at his best ; for that matter, no one who has ever drawn or painted him did so when he was at his best, for those moments came only in the seclusion of his own studio, when, alone with model or sitter, he worked absolutely oblivious to everything but his art. No man is at his best when posing for photograph, sketch, or portrait, and Whistler was farther from being an exception to this rule than most others. He knew too well what a portrait should be to feel the indifference which is essential to a perfectly natural pose. Consequently,

while few men were better known by sight in Paris
and London, scarce any one knew him as he was,—
the most profoundly serious, conscientious, and consistent artist of his day and generation.

As has been stated, he was always exceedingly
particular about his dress,—as finicky as a woman.
In his early London days he carried a long, slender
wand, like a mahl-stick, for a cane, and was conspicuous wherever he went, not only on account of his
diminutive size, but also by his stick and dress.

An attendant at an exhibition once wished to re-
lieve him of his cane, but he exclaimed :

"Oh, no, my man ! I keep this for the critics."

The following, by a London correspondent, is a
very good description, though of late years he had
abandoned the cane and his hair was somewhat
grayer :

"They say Whistler is fifty-six. But years have nothing
to do with him. He is as young in spirit, as lithe in body,
as dapper in 'get-up' as he was twenty years ago.

"Is there another man in London with such vitality as
Whistler has,—I care not what his age,—another so dainty,
another so sprightly in wit ? Do you see that dapper gentleman coming along Cheyne Walk, silk hat with very tall crown
and very straight brim ; habit apparently broadcloth (frock
coat), fitting to perfection a supple figure ; feet small as a
girl's,—an American girl's ; hands delicately gloved in yellow;
in the right hand a lithe, slim wand, twice as long as a walking stick ; glass in eye ; black moustache and slight 'imperial;'
black hair with wavy threads of gray here and there ? The
dainty gentleman lifts his hat, and you see above his forehead the slender, white lock—the white plume as famous as

OF JAMES A. McNEILL WHISTLER

that of Navarre. This is our friend Whistler, the inimitable, truly called 'the master.' You may meet him in the early morning, or at a private view in the afternoon, at an evening party, two hours before midnight or two hours after it ; and you will find him as fresh in spirit, as dainty, as lively, as witty at one time as at another.''

Some one once gave him an American umbrella,— one of those that when rolled tightly are as small as walking-sticks. He was delighted with it, and used it as a cane. One day, coming out of the studio with a friend, and while hurrying to the cab-stand a few blocks away, it began to drizzle, and his friend, who had no umbrella, said :

" Hurry and put up your umbrella or we'll get our hats wet."

He fumbled a second at the umbrella, then hurried on.

" But I would get my umbrella wet."

It was commonly said Whistler was unapproachable. In his studio, when at work, yes ; in his home, no.

A note of introduction from any approved correspondent would almost invariably bring a favorable response. But not every correspondent was approved ; or if so at one time, did not necessarily remain so indefinitely, and a note from the wrong—perhaps wronged—source was no commendation at all. On the whole, a frank application from a stranger for permission to call was quite as likely as not to prove successful, such a note in itself being a tribute.

But at the studio it was very different. He had no reception-days or hours, as many painters have. He had no use for the social rabble in his workshop.

One warm afternoon, when hard at work, the bell rang. Brush in hand, he went to the outer door at the head of the six flights of steep, slippery oak stairs, and found there Mr. C———, whom he knew,—a man who had little to do but bother others,—and Lady D———, a distinguished and clever woman, both out of breath from their long climb.

"Ah! my dear Mr. Whistler," drawled C———, "I have taken the liberty of bringing Lady D——— to see you. I knew you would be delighted."

"Delighted! I'm sure; quite beyond expression; but,"—mysteriously, and holding the door so as to bar their entrance,—"my dear Lady D———, I would never forgive our friend for bringing you up six flights of stairs on so hot a day to visit a studio at one of those—eh—pagan moments when"—and he glanced furtively behind him and still further closed the door—"it is absolutely impossible for a lady to be received. Upon my soul, I should never forgive him."

And the lady looked daggers at her confused cavalier, as Whistler bowed them down the six flights of oaken stairs and returned to resume work on the portrait of a very sedate old gentleman, who had taken advantage of the interruption to break for a moment the rigor of his pose.

In those days and for many years the Paris studio

was at No. 86 Notre Dame des Champs. Whistler
said one day, "Only the French have any taste in
the naming of streets."

The six steep flights of polished oak stairs no
doubt shortened his life by many years. As long
ago as 1894 he was accustomed to take a long rest
on a settee at the head of the third flight, and again
on reaching the top. Later he would have his
luncheon served in the studio to avoid the fatigue
of going down and coming back. He was by no
means an old man, and looked the picture of health,
cheeks ruddy, eye bright ; but he would get out of
breath, and his heart gave him trouble,—startled him
at times with its eccentricities and warnings.

A blunt friend, frightened at seeing him one day
almost collapse on reaching the studio, said :

"I tell you, Whistler, those stairs will be the
death of you ; and I'll be hanged if I am coming
here any more with you, for you'll die on my hands,
and that would get me into a nice mess. Why
don't you have a studio on the ground floor?"

"When I die—I will."

But while casual callers met with scant courtesy
at the studio, he was, as has already been noted,
exceptionally cordial to all who were sincerely interested in his work, and would spend hours and
hours of days that were precious in showing pictures
to people who really could not understand them,—
for that matter, who did understand them?—but
who were honest in their expressions of approval,

and this, too, with no thought of selling anything he had ; in fact, nothing chilled the enthusiasm of the moment so much as the suggestion of a purchase ; he became immediately a different being, and one by one his treasures would be turned to the wall.

The studio was a large barn-like room at the very top of the high building.   There was a small entry-way, which had a glass door opening out upon a balcony, high up over the street, and another door which opened into the studio proper.

A huge skylight lighted this great attic, but only in part, for the room was too big to be well lighted from any one opening.

The old oak floor was quite dark, and in places where he worked it was polished by use, for when entirely absorbed he had the habit of moving back and forth so quickly as to slide a pace or two.

The tone of the studio was brown, not a deep or muddy brown, but a brown that seemed tinged with gray.

The base-board that stretched a narrow line about the big room was a deeper shade than the wall, and so nice were the gradations of tone, that floor, base-board, wall, and raftered ceiling blended together as one harmonious whole, all of which was the work of Whistler.

The furniture amounted to nothing : a table near the far side, where he lunched, an old sofa against the wall under the skylight, two or three old French chairs, his easel and palette.   There was a high stove near the door,—one of those French complications intended for the generation of a maximum of heat with a minimum consumption of precious coal. Like most labor-saving devices, it required some skill for its management, and Whistler was not a mechanic.

One cold day it was only too apparent the stove needed encouragement, and the sitter suggested that the damper be opened,—in fact, started to open it himself, when Whistler, greatly alarmed, exclaimed :

" God bless me ! but you must not touch that ; the last time I meddled with it, the fire went out. There is only one man in Paris who understands that stove."

" Well, where is he ?"

" Dear me, I discharged him to-day. How unlucky."

" Then, we must seize the stove by the horns and take our chances on the consequences." And throwing the damper wide open, there was soon a blazing fire.

For work outside, Whistler used a very small palette of the usual form ; in his studio he carried no palette whatsoever, but used in lieu thereof a rectangular table that resembled a writing-desk. The top sloped slightly ; at the left were tubes of colors, at the right one or two bowls containing oil and turpentine, with which the colors when mixed were reduced so thin that they would run on the sloping top of the table.

He relied upon innumerable coats of thin color to secure the desired effect rather than upon one or two coats of greater consistency. This made the work long and tedious as compared with the modern mode of taking the pigments as they squirm from the tubes and pasting them while yet alive on the canvas; but it has undoubtedly given his pictures a permanency and durability far beyond that of others.

He seldom began to arrange his palette until the model or sitter was in pose; and ten or fifteen minutes were not infrequently spent in getting palette and brushes to suit him. To a model paid by the hour this delay was of no concern, but to the unpractised sitter, whose limit of endurance and patience did not exceed an hour, the time spent in setting the palette seemed unduly long and altogether wasted. But all that was a part of the refinement of Whistler's art.

So susceptible was his color-sense that he could not mix colors to suit him unless canvas and sitter were before him precisely as they would be when he began to paint. The arrangement of the colors on the palette was but preliminary to placing those same colors on the canvas, therefore the sitter was as essential to the one process as the other.

Once inside his studio, Whistler seemed to lose all the eccentricities of manner by which he was known to the world. He doffed his coat, substituted for his monocle a pair of servicable spectacles, and was ready for work.

If it were a full-length portrait, he placed the canvas near his palette and his sitter in pose about four feet to the other side of the easel. For observation he stood about twelve feet back towards the doorway,—very close, in fact, to the refractory stove. The light fell slanting on the right of the portrait and sitter, over the painter's left shoulder, and this light he would modify each day according to the amount of sunshine and the effect he desired.

He then selected two or three small brushes with handles about three feet in length, stood back about twelve feet, took a good look at both sitter and canvas, then stepping quickly forward, and, standing as far from the canvas as the long handles and his arms permitted, he began to rapidly sketch in the figure with long, firm strokes of the brush. The advantage of long handles was obvious,—they enabled him to stand back quite a distance and sketch directly from his sitter. Except for this first sketch, he used ordinary brushes with ordinary handles.

There was nothing eccentric or unusual in his methods or in what he worked with. Probably no painter in all Paris used simpler means to arrive at great results. It is quite likely that no other painter of to-day—judging entirely from appearances of modern canvases—could achieve any satisfactory results with materials so elemental.

To make the sketch required possibly thirty minutes. To the casual observer there was often more of a likeness in the first sketch than at any time after,—which simply goes to show the power of line devoid of color and also the easy task of the caricaturist.

The sketch finished, the long-handled brushes were discarded and work began in earnest. With one or more, sometimes a handful of brushes,—for they would accumulate without his realizing it,—he would again stand back and carefully scrutinize sitter and canvas until it seemed as if—and no doubt it was so—he transferred a visual impression of the subject to the canvas and fixed it there ready to be made permanent with line and color ; then quickly, often with a run and a slide, he rushed up to the canvas and, without glancing at his sitter, vigorously painted so long as his visual image lasted, then going back the full distance he took another look, and so on day after day to the end.

In life-size work he seldom stood close to the canvas and painted direct from his sitter.

He has laid down the proposition :

" The one aim of the unsuspecting painter is to make his man ' stand out' from the frame, never doubting that, on the contrary, he should really, and in truth absolutely does, stand *within* the frame, and at a depth behind it equal to the distance at which the painter sees his model. The frame is, indeed, the window through which the painter looks at his model, and nothing could be more offensively inartistic than this brutal attempt to thrust the model on the hitherside of this window." [1]

---

[1] Gentle Art, pp. 177, 178.

OF JAMES A. McNEILL WHISTLER

The number of sittings required varied greatly, and did not depend in any degree upon the size of the canvas. Sometimes he would paint a life-size figure with great rapidity ; again he would spend weeks and months on a very small picture. All depending upon conditions over which he had no control.

He has devoted as many as ninety sittings to a portrait, only to pronounce it unfinished and unsatisfactory.

No work counted or was permitted to remain save that painted in what he called his "grand manner," which meant the work of those days and hours when everything—sitter, light, weather, spirits, mood, enthusiasm—was just right,—a combination that might come several days in succession or but once in a fortnight.

He once said, "The portrait of my mother was painted in a few hours," meaning that the work of the last few hours was the work that really counted.

It was interesting to watch a picture grow under the hands of Whistler. With most painters something is finished from day to day, and in the course of ten or twelve sittings the portrait is complete. Not so with him. Nothing, not a detail, not even an infinitesimal section of the background was finished until the last.

He worked with great rapidity and long hours, but he used his colors thin and covered the canvas with innumerable coats of paint. The colors increased in depth and intensity as the work progressed. At first the entire figure was painted in grayish-brown tones, with very little of flesh color, the whole blending perfectly with the grayish-brown of the prepared canvas ; then the entire background would be intensified a little ; then the figure made a little stronger ; then the background, and so on from day to day and week to week, and often from month to month, to the exhaustion of the sitter, but the perfection of the work, if the sitter remained patient and continued in favor.

At no time did he permit the figure to get away from or out of the background ; at no time did he permit the background to oppress the figure, but the development of both was even and harmonious, with neither discord nor undue contrast.

And so the portrait would really grow, really develop as an entirety, very much as a negative under the action of the chemicals comes out gradually—lights, shadows, and all from the first faint indications to their full values.

It was as if the portrait were hidden within the canvas and the master by passing his wands day after day over the surface evoked the image.

Most painters can take a canvas and begin at once with the colors of the finished picture, making each stroke count from the very first, often, if the canvas has been prepared, doing little or nothing to the background. Whistler himself would sometimes let the prepared canvas show, all the resources of his art he understood, but if he did, the picture was simply a sketch.

OF JAMES A. McNEILL WHISTLER

In a very profound sense Whistler's work from the very beginning was always finished,—finished in the sense that any growing thing is perfect from day to day. The plant may be but a tender shoot just appearing above the ground, or it may be in full leaf, or in gorgeous blossom, but it is finished, it is perfect by day and night. In that sense were Whistler's paintings finished. If they were sketches, then the slight amount of color used was precisely the amount the sketch required. At no time was the sense of proportion outraged by carrying line or color or likeness beyond the symmetrical development of the three.

One must not be understood as saying that all his pictures are of equal merit,—perfection does not necessarily mean that ; nor that he did not do many things he considered failures.

Few painters ever destroyed more work, no painter was ever more critical of his own work. But, in spite of all he could do, things would get out into the world that he wished destroyed. This was due in part to the facility with which he made sketches and the enthusiasm with which he would begin new things, many of which never got on. Now and then some of these unfinished things— unfinished from the first stroke, because never quite satisfactory to him—would escape his studio.

Artists express very positive opinions regarding the merits of his pictures, placing some with the best the world has done, others as quite unworthy the master. As no two painters agree which are the best and which are the least worthy, the layman is helpless. In truth, only Whistler himself could have pointed out all the qualities and defects, and this he never did. If pressed for an opinion or a preference, he would evade the question, or by deftly speaking of this or that quality of the works under discussion would leave his hearers with the impression they knew all about the matter, when in reality they were no wiser than before. He simply did not care to discuss his work intimately with the lay or the professional mind. What he saw was beyond their comprehension, or if not beyond their comprehension, then they saw it without further words from him, for did not the picture speak plainly for itself?

Contrary to general impression, he was patience itself in his studio. A sitter who was with him every day for nearly six weeks never heard him utter an impatient word; on the contrary, he was all kindness. He would permit his sitter to bring friends to the studio, and he would listen to all the foolish suggestions that could occur to a tired and impatient man.

Sometimes he would rebuke a too-insistent sitter, as the following anecdotes show, if true :

It is said that one man annoyed him by saying at the end of each sitting :

" How about that ear, Mr. Whistler? Don't forget to finish that !"

At the last sitting, everything being done except this ear, Whistler said :

"Well, I think I am through. Now I'll sign it." Which he did in a very solemn, important manner, as was his way.

"But my ear, Mr. Whistler ! You aren't going to leave it that way?"

"Oh, you can put it in after you get home."

He was once painting the portrait of a distinguished novelist, who, though extremely clever, was not blessed with the fatal gift of beauty. When the portrait was finished, the sitter did not seem satisfied with it.

"Don't you like it?" inquired Whistler.

"No ; can't say I do. But," in self justification, "you must admit that it is a bad work of art."

"Yes," Whistler replied ; "but I think you must admit that you are a bad work of nature."

The truth is, he would listen to every suggestion made by the sitter, model, or even casual visitor, if one were admitted.

A sitter once said to him :

"Mr. Whistler, isn't there something wrong about the right eye?"

Instantly alert, he said :

"What's that you say? Um—um—right eye——" And he carefully examined the canvas. "We'll have a look at that. Suppose you stand for just a moment —just a moment." And he paid as much heed as if the criticism had come from competent sources.

Mrs. Whistler would now and then come to the

studio, and he would eagerly ask her opinion of the progress made ; and her suggestions were always followed. For her ability as an artist—for her own pleasure, rather than for profit—and as a critic of his work he had the highest opinion. Her suggestions were ever to the point, and under her influence a work always made rapid headway. It was an irreparable loss when she died in 1897, and he was never again quite so light-hearted. For a long time he kept the apartments at 110 Rue du Bac, but did not live there.

His will expressed his devotion to her memory and belief in her art,—

" I bequeath my wife's entire collection of garnets rare and beautiful, together with sprays, pendants, etc., of the same style of work or setting in white stones, brilliants, or old paste, our entire collection of beautiful old silver and plate, and the complete collection of old china, to the Louvre. This bequest is on condition that the three collections be gathered together in one and displayed as the ' Beatrix Whistler Collection.' Also that in it or appropriately in the same room shall be hung proofs of my wife's exquisite etchings, of which I leave a list attached to my will signed by me."

By a codicil dated May 7, 1903, he revoked the bequest to the Louvre, but he expressed a desire that, in the event of his residuary legatee retaining the collection of garnets during her life, she would bequeath them to the Louvre upon her death.

He was unsparing of his sitters only in this one respect,—he would become so absorbed in his work as to completely forget them, and they would collapse with fatigue. Sometimes he would notice by their pallor the faintness which was overcoming them, and instantly, all solicitude, he would have them rest, or go out on the balcony for fresh air ; but he himself never sat down. While they were resting he would walk back and forth, looking at the canvas, but rarely touching it, and talking to himself,—now and then, but not often, taking the sitter into his confidence. The moment the sitter was rested he would begin working again like one possessed.

By close observation it could be seen that the best work was usually done during the first long pose, or in the last hour of the afternoon, when the shadows were deepening ; and the wise sitter would humor this trait and pose his longest and best in those two hours.

To the unaccustomed a half-hour standing—without moving so much as to disturb a line of the garments—is a long pose. But with practice—and with Whistler one had practice—an hour and a half without moving a muscle is not impossible.

Every portrait Whistler ever began he expected to make his masterpiece. That is the way he started in with any work. It was to be the best thing he ever did ; and so long as the enthusiasm lasted he would walk up and down the studio talking half to himself half to his sitter :

" We will just go right on as we have begun, and it will be fine,—perhaps the finest thing I have ever done."

" Not as good as the portrait of your mother?" —the inevitable question.

" Perhaps ; who knows ?   Possibly finer in a way ; for this, you know, is different.   We'll make a big thing of it."   And so on for days and weeks, until something would occur,—possibly weariness on the part of the sitter ; possibly failure to keep appointments on days when the painter felt like doing his best ; possibly too great anxiety to see the picture finished,—and the painter's enthusiasm would subside, and the portrait would turn out not so great after all.

After the first few days he would place the canvas in its frame, and thereafter paint with it so.   And his frames were designed by himself.   All who have seen his pictures know them,—just simple, dignified lines, with no contortions of wood and gilt.

When a sitter was of congenial spirit and complacent mood they would lunch in the studio, and he would paint all day, from eleven in the morning until—well, until it was so dark that all was dim and shadowy and ghostly ; and then together both would take their leave, always turning at the door for a last look at the canvas looming mysterious in the darkness ; then grope their way down the winding oaken stairs, later to dine together at some unfrequented place where the proprietor watched the

OF JAMES A. McNEILL WHISTLER

fire himself and had stored away in musty depths a few—just a few—relics of memorable vintages.

" O my friends, when I am sped, appoint a meeting ; and when ye have met together, be ye glad thereof ; and when the cup-bearer holds in her hand a flagon of old wine, then think of old Khayyam and drink to his memory."

In a glass of ruby Margaux of the vintage of '58, the last of its dusty bin, I drink to the memory of those glorious days when the vacant canvas assumed the hues of life and grew beneath the touch ; and those fragrant nights when, with stately ceremony, the cob-webbed bottle came forth from its bed of long repose to subdue fatigue, banish all care, and leave but the thought of the beautiful.— Behold, far soul, the empty glass !

RECOLLECTIONS AND IMPRESSIONS

IX

Portrait-Painting — How he Differed from his Great Predecessors — The "Likeness" — Composition of Color — No Commercial Side — Baronet vs. Butterfly.

WHISTLER was not a "portrait-painter," as the phrase goes nowadays ; but he was, in certain respects, the greatest painter of portraits the world has known.

As a "portrait-painter" he fell far short of Rembrandt, Velasquez, and a host of lesser men ; but as a painter of portraits he rose superior to them all in certain refinements of the art.

There is a vast difference between the "portrait-painter" to whom the sitter is of first importance and the painter to whom his art is of first importance. The difference lies in the attitude of the artist towards his canvas, towards the work he is about to undertake. Is the inspiration wholly his own, or is he influenced by considerations quite foreign to the production of a pure work of art?

The attitude of the "portrait-painter" may be likened unto that of the "poet laureate," whose verse is at the command of conditions he does not control ; who *may*, by accident, write a good thing,— but the rule is otherwise, with even the best.

To rightly place a human being on canvas, or in stone, or in marble, or in poetry, is the noblest achievement of art. On the technical side it exhausts the resources of the art ; on the spiritual side it exhausts the genius of the artist. But "portrait-painting" as a profession, as an industrial and a commercial proposition, is a degradation of art. It is in strict accord with the spirit of the age ; it is a natural and an inevitable evolution. But it is, nevertheless, a degradation,—for wherein does the shop-like atelier of the professional "portrait-painter" differ from the emporium and the bazaar of commerce ? And wherein do the methods of the shrewd and successful painter differ from those of the successful merchant ? Are not the doors of the studio open to every comer with a purse? Are not the prices fixed at so much per square yard of canvas? Is not the patronage of celebrities sought, regardless of artistic possibilities, for the prestige it gives? Are not the A. R. A. and the R. A., and all the degrees and decorations, sought, like the "By special appointment to H. M. —" of the tradesman, for the money there is in them?

But what need to enumerate the motives that move the professional "portrait-painter,"—they are written on his every canvas.

Sculpture still clings to its ideals, and the "bust-maker" is a term of reproach. No sculptor with any ambition whatsoever, with any love for his art, would willingly look forward to a career of portrait bust-making. Dire necessity may compel him, and year after year he may make the marble and bronze effigies of local celebrities ; but the yoke galls, the task wearies, and he looks forward to the time when, emancipated from his thraldom, he may do something *of his own*.

Not so the "portrait-painter." He glories in his degradation ; paints a score of huge, staring canvases, blatant likenesses of blatant people, and, before the paint is dry, parades them in exhibition as his latest galaxy of masterpieces,—not that his art may be magnified, but that his trade may be advertised.

The sculptor is only too glad if his bronze effigies are hidden in leafy thickets, in parks, and out-of-the-way places. He has not learned the commercial value of exhibitions. He does not every few months place on view a lot of marbles and bronzes, the work of as many weeks. He has not caught from the shop-keeper the trick of displaying his wares in a window. But the "portrait-painter"—— !

"Portrait-painting" pays,—that is the worst of it all. It is the one branch of the art of painting that can be followed as methodically as the making of clothes. It is, for that matter, closely allied to and quite dependent upon the tailor and the dressmaker. Worth made more portraits than any painter of the day in Paris.

The "portrait-painter" must dress his manikin in clothes that will "paint," for the manikin is worse than nothing for the picture. There must be a gown of brilliant stuffs, and either a hat or the hair-dresser,—who also has made and unmade portraits,—or there must be a uniform, hunting-breeches, judge's gown and wig, accordingly as the manikin is woman or man ; and it is the theatrical trappings that are painted, and, incidentally thereto, —manikin.

Reynolds painted something like two thousand canvases. In 1758 one hundred and fifty persons sat to him,—an average of three portraits a week. He was as methodical as an automatic machine. Rose early, breakfasted at nine, was in the studio at ten, worked by himself until eleven, when his first sitter of the day would appear, to be succeeded by another precisely one hour later, and so on, a sitter an hour, until four o'clock, when the popular painter made himself ready for a plunge in the social swirl.

Portraits produced under such conditions cannot be made more than technically brilliant,—superficial likenesses of the great majority of the sitters,—and are unworthy the painter's art.

After a brief study of their careers, and without seeing a portrait by either, one would be warranted in looking for a masterpiece among Gainsborough's two hundred and twenty portraits rather than among the two thousand canvases of Reynolds.

Great facility of execution is not necessarily a

condemnatory feature of a man's art, but it is a dangerous feature, and with most men it is a fatal feature.

The hand of the master must be entirely subservient to the brain. No obstacle should intervene between the inspiration and its complete expression, but the hand must not force the imagination ; and it is true that command of technic—mere digital dexterity—does lead the performer, whether painter or musician, to speak when he has nothing to say.

Happily for the reputation of Reynolds, he painted now and then a portrait in which he took more interest, and these have some—possibly not many —of the qualities that live. For the most part his reputation rests on mere volume of brilliant and high-grade work,—very much as one factory has a greater reputation than another. And he did more than any man who ever lived to reduce " portrait-painting" to a trade, a mechanical pursuit.

In the modern sense of the phrase, he was one of the greatest of " portrait-painters ;" certainly the most " successful"—again in the modern sense— the world has known, of talent supreme, in genius wanting.

But there are portraits and portraits,—to illustrate :

There are portraits.

There are portraits that are also pictures.

There are pictures that are also portraits.

There are pictures.

248

The first-named are mere likenesses,—photographs on canvas. This sort is very common and very popular ; they are made with great facility by the professional " portrait-painters" and they are greatly applauded wherever seen. They have their fixed prices,—so much for half, three-quarters, or full-length,—and they are quite a matter of commerce, with a maximum of dexterity and a minimum of art. There are those who can and do paint great portraits, who turn out endless numbers of these mechanically-made things to the detriment of their art. Of the best of this sort were the most of Reynolds's portraits,—superficially brilliant and attractive likenesses that ought not to be seen outside the family circle for which they were intended. Of this same sort are most of those startling people who issue from the studios of the popular " portrait-painters" of to-day, to thrust the nonentity of their individualities upon us. The identity of the " Blue-Boy," by Gainesborough, is quite immaterial ; the identity of the " Shrimp-Girl," by Hogarth, is likewise immaterial ; the identity of the " Child with a Sword," by Manet, is of no importance,—for these are pictures, though at the same time portraits.

But the identity of the " portraits" by the popular " portrait-painter" is, in ninety-nine instances out of a hundred, a matter of great importance, the value of the canvas being enhanced by the celebrity or notoriety of the sitter.

The mere portrait is better than no portrait at all, but it should be a fixture in its own household, a family heirloom, and strictly entailed ; descendants failing, then to the midden.

Between the mere portrait and the portrait that possesses some of the universal qualities of a work of art the interval is wide, and almost one of kind rather than degree, though no line of strict demarcation can be drawn ; while, as between the painting that is primarily a portrait, with incidental universal qualities, and a painting that is primarily a work of art, and incidentally a portrait, the difference is entirely a matter of degree.

In, for instance, the "Blue-Boy" the portrait element predominates ; in the "Shrimp-Girl" the universal element predominates. In the former, the portrait was uppermost in the painter's mind ; in the other, the picture was the only consideration. And yet Hogarth's is undoubtedly the more perfect portrait, though slight and sketchy as compared with the composition and finish of the Gainsborough.

In fact, the "Shrimp-Girl," as an abstract work of art, is a degree higher than the picture-portrait. It is a picture,—a work of art in the doing of which no considerations other than the artistic intention moved the painter.

A mere portrait, in the dash and brilliancy of its execution or the decorative quality of its color, may be better than a picture of indifferent execution or poor color ; the one may be worth keeping in a limited circle, or even of some use decoratively in a more general way, while the other is not worth preserving at all. But there is hope for the man who attempts to paint a picture, to produce a work of art, though he fails miserably ; whereas there is no hope for the brilliant technician whose sole ambition is to paint and sell his canvas photographs as rapidly as possible.

Manet's "Child with a Sword" is a superb portrait of a child,—a model, to be sure, but none the less a little human being, with as many attributes of life and humanity as the child whose parents pay the price of a likeness. Manet's chief merit lies in the fact that all his life long he tried to paint pictures, sometimes successfully, sometimes unsuccessfully ; never with any profound insight into human nature or life, but always straightforwardly and sincerely, and with a strong, firm hand. He painted many portraits of his sister and his friends, but invariably with the intention to do something of more universal validity than a likeness.

The casual visitor to the Louvre may examine at his leisure the little "Infanta" and the "Mona Lisa," both great pictures, both great portraits, but of the two the portrait element is rather more pronounced in the Velasquez than in the Leonardo.

The little "Infanta" is there for all time on the canvas, precisely as she was in the painter's studio, a wonderful portrait of a child, a wonderful picture of a bit of humanity, but less of a type than an individual.

As for the "Mona Lisa," who can doubt that in the long years the painter worked on this portrait all superficial resemblances and characteristics disappeared until the constant, the elemental, the soul alone remained? It possesses many of the qualities of the idealized madonnas of Italian religious art. It began with the painter's admiration of a beautiful woman, an individual of that day and generation; it ended with an ideal which will last so long as the slowly-darkening pigments retain line and lineaments.

The mere adding of accessories in the way of composition or background or the adoption of a classic or theatrical pose may make the work more decorative, but it does not enhance the real merit of the portrait, the status of which cannot be altered by the surrounding canvas.

When Mrs. Siddons entered Reynolds's studio, he said, as he conducted her to the raised platform :·

"Take your seat upon the throne for which you were born, and suggest to me the idea of the 'Tragic Muse.'"

"I made a few steps," relates the actress, "and then took at once the attitude in which the 'Tragic Muse' has remained."

When the portrait was finished, Sir Joshua said :

"I cannot lose this opportunity of sending my name to posterity on the hem of your garment," and he placed his signature on the border of the gown.

All of which are the conditions under which theatrical and meritricious art is produced. The portrait of a woman posing as the "Tragic Muse" *may* turn out well, but the chances are otherwise.

OF JAMES A. McNEILL WHISTLER

There are "portrait-painters" who are better than others, and the best of all were Rembrandt and Velasquez, the latter the greatest portrait-painter who ever lived,—so great that his portraits are great as pictures ; but not quite in the abstract sense that a painting by Raphael is a picture,—a bright and beautiful song in line and color ; not quite in the sense that a painting by Angelo is a picture,—the tumultuous outpouring of a human soul ; not quite in the subtle sense that a painting by Whistler is a picture,—a harmony to delight the eye as music delights the ear.

Rembrandt and Velasquez were great in technical directions in their portraiture, and their achievements remain unchallenged ; but in the painting of portraits each was something of the "portrait-painter,"—not the facile, commercial painter of to-day, but they painted portraits to earn their living. Now and then the portrait was a labor of love and a great picture, seldom—at least in the case of Velasquez—a matter of drudgery, and therefore a failure.

Velasquez was so happily situated in the court at Madrid, of the king's household, on friendly terms with the royal family, that he painted their portraits with far more devotion and interest than he could possibly feel towards a stranger.

A portrait of Philip the Fourth by Velasquez ought to be as good a work of art as a bust of Pericles by Phidias,—and that is about the most that can be said in portraiture,—but a bust of

RECOLLECTIONS AND IMPRESSIONS

Pericles would not be the best that the art of
Phidias could do, for his art was not limited by
lineaments.

Wherein the art of Whistler differed from the art
of Rembrandt and Velasquez in the painting of
human likenesses is as follows :

With Whistler the sitter, whether model or patron,
was subordinated to the composition, to the harmony of line and color,—was simply an integral part
of the larger scheme in the painter's mind.

With Rembrandt and Velasquez the sitter was
the important feature, everything else being quite
casual ; the object in mind being to paint a great
portrait, to put a human being on canvas. A worthy
object when worthily done, but not quite so pure
and subtle and abstract, not quite so free from limitations of time and place and person as the intention
to do something of universal validity in which the
individual shall not obtrude beyond his due measure
of importance.

In the attempt to do things that had never been
done before, in the attempt to make painting as pure
an art as music and poetry, Whistler possibly made
many failures, or rather many more or less incom-
plete successes, but in his best things it is undeniably
true that he produced pictures wherein the portrait
element was as subtly if not as "strongly" developed
as in anything ever before painted, and wherein at
the same time that element was successfully subordinated to ideals more refined and universal.

OF JAMES A. McNEILL WHISTLER

Both Rembrandt and Velasquez did "stronger" things than Whistler,—that is to say, they placed their subjects more positively and forcefully on the canvas, so that they stand out more aggressively, and fill not only their frames but the room ; they do not obtrude, but they are great big characterizations which make themselves felt in any company.

Whistler's portraits, like all his pictures, retire within their frames, do not assert themselves, are not "strong," as the term is quite legitimately used in the sense of powerful, positive, and vigorous. His portraits are neither "stunning" nor overwhelming ; they are so quiet, restful, and harmonious as to almost escape notice. There is a wraith-like quality about some of them that has often been noted ; some of them seem the portraits of shadows rather than realities.

A woman standing before "The Fur Jacket" said :
" So that is a portrait of a woman by Whistler?"
" No," replied her companion ; " it is Whistler's impression of a woman."

Neither was right,—for, as a matter of fact, it is simply a composition of line and color wherein a woman—in this case a model—is the central figure of the arrangement. The painting of a likeness was not in Whistler's mind at all. The painting of a woman, either as a type or an individual, probably did not enter his head ; but he had in mind a scheme which pleased him, and this scheme he placed on canvas. It is quite likely the woman happened to enter his studio, and the effect of figure, costume, and environment caught his fancy. That was the way many of the portraits were begun.

Lady Archibald Campbell was nothing to him except a possibility ; she was to him as a theme, as a motive to a musician. At the outset he had all sorts of trouble with the picture ; and it was not until one day Lady Campbell happened to come in with her fur cape over her shoulders that he made a new start and painted the picture. It is a great portrait, one of his very best, a haunting likeness of a woman ; not such a photographic likeness as friends and relatives demand, but just the likeness that posterity demands : a woman, a type, with all the charm, all the refinement, all the real, the true, the elusive qualities of a woman,—in short, those qualities of mind and body which reappear in descendants of the third and fourth generation and demonstrate the faithfulness of the portrait.

There is no portrait by Rembrandt or Velasquez which at all resembles Whistler's portrait of his mother.

It is not at all like anything by Rembrandt ; there is a hint of the blacks and grays of Velasquez, but that is a superficial observation made by every passing tourist.

In scheme, composition, intention, and execution the picture is essentially different from anything the great Spanish painter ever did. One ought to recognize the fundamental difference between the two artists on looking at the little " Infanta" in the

Louvre,—there is no need to go farther. Velasquez had a firm strong grasp of life about him which Whistler lacked. The one was a man among men, the other a poet among poets, a musician among musicians, a dreamer among dreamers ; the one painted men, women, and children because they interested him, the other painted them because he was interested in beautiful things ; the one viewed the world by day with his feet planted firmly on the ground, the other viewed it by dusk and by night with his head in the mist and clouds.

There was the same difference between Velasquez and Whistler that there is between two poets, one of whom—like, say, Byron—deals with life with a sure hand, the other—like Keats—deals with beauty as the finest thing in life.

In poetry even the casual reader does not confound men of opposite temperaments, though both use the medium of verse to express their thoughts ; but in painting, people habitually confuse men who have absolutely nothing in common except the medium they use. And yet for every poet there is somewhere a painter of like moods and temperament. Men do not differ, though some use poetry, some music, some sculpture, some painting to express their fancies and convictions.

Were one so disposed, it would not be difficult to point out the Browning, the Tennyson, the Whitman, the Bach, the Beethoven, the Wagner of painting, for the human soul is the same in every art.

RECOLLECTIONS AND IMPRESSIONS

Beyond the fact, therefore, that Velasquez and Whistler both expressed themselves by means of painting, they were not at all alike, and their work must reflect their fundamental differences.

Whistler, in susceptibility to color and fleeting line, in love for abstract, almost ethereal beauty, was akin to the choice spirits of the far East. He found more that appealed to him and affected him in the blue-and-white porcelain of China than in any painting from Madrid. Velasquez might give him many valuable hints as to the use of color, as to the practice of his art, but no suggestions whatsoever as to ends and aims. These motives he found in the East, in those wonderful lands where men, leaving nature far behind, almost touched heaven in their philosophies, and did seize some of heaven's infinite blues and silvery grays in their arts.

It is idle to compare Whistler's portraits with those of any other man, for the qualities that make those of others great are not found accentuated in his, and the qualities that make his great are not found refined in those of others.

The matter of likeness, which troubles most people, is of vital importance to the " portrait-painter," since it is his sole excuse, the only justification he has for existing, but to art it does not matter at all.

Likeness has no objective existence. It is entirely a matter of impression, a subjective realiza-

tion. Beyond the size of the mouth, the shape of
the nose, the color of the eyes there is little to
what is called a "likeness." A person never looks
the same to different people or on different occasions.

To the casual acquaintance a "likeness" is but
skin deep ; to the friend of a lifetime it is altogether a matter of character. A portrait that
satisfies a wife fails to please a mother, and one that
provokes the applause of the passing throng is a
disappointment to the family.

For what is one man's appearance to another but
the impact of personality upon personality, the
coming together of two vitalities clothed in flesh
and blood. But some there are who see only the
clothes of another,—the very outward shell and
husk ; others who see only the flesh and blood,—
the physical covering ; others who get at the man
and know him in part as he is. For whom shall the
portrait be painted,—for those who see, or those
who know, or those who love? And by whom
shall the portrait be painted,—by the tailor-painter
or by the soul-painter?

The world is filled with painters of the superficial, with painters of husks ; and those are the
painters who impress the multitude, for they see
what the multitude see, and there is no mystery to
puzzle, but everything is superficial and plain.

A likeness is the physical semblance of the soul ;
and the only likeness worth having on canvas or in

marble or in words is the faithful transcript of the impression the sitter makes on the artist.

From the fact that this impression changes and deepens from hour to hour, and day to day, and week to week, as the two beings come to know each other, it follows that the best portrait can only be painted after sufficient acquaintance for the dissipation of those superficial traits and characteristics which envelop everyone like a fog.

It is the special province of caricature to seize upon a man's superficialities and peculiarities, and make the most or the worst of them ; but it is the business of portraiture to get beneath and give a glimpse, an impression of the true man.

To this end Whistler's many and long sittings were of inestimable service. The portrait grew with his acqaintance with his sitter. What first pleased him as a scheme of color and an agreeable personality came in time to interest him as a human being, with the result in the most successful canvases that the picture would be all he desired as a harmony, as a song without sound, and also a marvellously subtle realization of his impression of the human being he had learned to know.

In one respect the identity of a portrait is not a matter of entire indifference, for the attitude of the painter is more or less affected by his relation to the sitter, and whatever affects him affects his work.

Many an artist does his best when his wife or child or some one he loves is the model ; and the man who could not paint his mother a little better, a little more sympathetically than a stranger would be soulless indeed. In poetry the influence of a mistress is a matter of tradition.

The picture, as a work of art, must be judged independently of its associations. It stands by itself, and is good, bad, or indifferent, regardless of the painter or the conditions under which it was done ; but some of its excellencies may be explained if we learn it was a labor of love.

It would not add a feather's weight to the superb qualitities of the " Hermes," at Olympia, if it were discovered to be a likeness of the sculptor's son ; nor would it detract in the slightest degree from its perfection if it were found to have been the work of an unknown man, and not by Praxiteles,— though in the latter case there would be a great abatement of enthusiasm on the part of the touring public. But if a number of the master's works were in existence, and it was perceived that the " Hermes" possessed certain qualities of tenderness, certain indefinable elements of superiority that made it the masterpiece, the knowledge that some one whom the sculptor loved dearly had posed would help to explain the almost imperceptible differences. The work would stand on its own merits ; but one of the reasons why it stood so high would be found in the relationship between sculptor and model.

By many who should be qualified to speak Whistler's portrait of his mother is considered his masterpiece, possibly by some because it is of his mother, but by others quite independently of the relationship.

Others there are who consider the portrait of Carlyle his masterpiece, possibly because it is of Carlyle, but by some independently of the identity of the sitter.

Seldom is the portrait of any unknown or less known sitter mentioned in comparison,—all of which goes to show the bias which results from knowing the identity.

Every Scotchman would insist upon the Carlyle, most of them quite unconscious of the patriotic bias.

There are pictures far more subtle in color, more "Whistlerian" in effect, more distinctively the creations of a great poet in color than these two portraits, but as compared with any *two*, or even *three*, or, possibly, *four* others, the preservation of these are of vital importance to the fame of the artist and the advancement of art. In this sense they may be considered his masterpieces, and of the two the one that hangs in the Luxembourg is far the finer. It is one of the few pictures that leave nothing to be said by painter or layman.

It is more than a portrait,—it is a large composition of line and form and color ; it is a great portrait made subordinate to a great picture.

Whistler was seldom so satisfied with a portrait that he was willing to part with it. He could always see things he wished to change,—partly, no doubt, because his impression of his subject changed from day to day,—and he would often keep a portrait by him for months and years before exhibiting. In fact he exhibited a like reserve about nearly all his work. It was next to impossible to get anything from him for current exhibitions.

He would faithfully and with the best of intentions promise to have something ready. The time would come, and he would be found still at work on the canvas as leisurely as if so many centuries were before him instead of so many hours. Nothing ever induced him to either hasten his work or exhibit it unfinished. The fact that he might not be represented gave him not the slightest uneasiness. The result was that the Whistlers seen were generally old Whistlers,—all the better for that. For instance, of the pictures exhibited at the World's Columbian Exposition, not one had been painted within ten or fifteen years,—two dated as far back as 1864.

At the Antwerp Exhibition, a year later, there was certainly not a picture painted within ten years. By this method the artist had the advantage of his own mature judgment and the assistance of time,—and time wields a great brush. There is no glaze, no finish, no varnish equal to that dispensed so evenly, so mellowly, so softly, so beautifully by time. Furthermore, there is no judgment so sound, no criticism so penetrating as the judgment and criticism of the artist himself on his own work after the enthusiasm of the hour has worn off. One of the finest indications of Whistler's greatness was this reserve in the exhibition of new work, this ability to do fine things and quietly put them away out of sight, until with lapse of time they could be looked over dispassionately, repainted if necessary, and either banished forever or exhibited in all their glory.

Most artists delight in seeing exhibited immediately—often prematurely—the things they do, and the delight is not unnatural. Others there are who, on account of numerous disappointments or from queer crotchets, are opposed altogether to exhibitions. Whistler was not of the latter class ; he was quite human enough to enjoy, as he himself said, the honors which come from well-conducted exhibitions. He was an officer of the Legion of Honor, had received awards and honors without number, including the extraordinary award of the gold medal for etching and also for painting at the Paris Exposition of 1900, and an honorary degree from a Scotch University. These honors sat lightly, but by no means uneasily, upon him.

His unwillingness to part with work led to no end of trouble and misunderstanding. People could not understand why they should not have what they had bargained and often paid for, why there should be any delay whatsoever, much less why after many demands their money should be returned and the picture kept by the artist.

OF JAMES A. McNEILL WHISTLER

All this is, of course, diametrically opposed to the rules of commerce, and Whistler has been blamed for his unreliability, to use the mildest term urged against him.

Without knowing him it is impossible to understand his attitude towards his pictures.

In the first place, he was profoundly attached to them, whether sold or not. They were and remained *his* work ; and in a humorous way he frequently insisted upon this superior right of the creator,—as on the fly-leaf of the catalogue of his London exhibition, which read :

" *Nocturnes, Marines, and Chevalet Pieces :* a catalogue. Small collection kindly *lent* their owners."

And sometimes this assertion of a superior equity went so far as to interfere with the right of possession, which was quite beyond the comprehension of the multitude.

The story is told that a certain Lady B—— purchased one of his pictures, but was never able to get it.

One day she drove to the studio in her victoria. Mr. Whistler went out to the sidewalk to greet her.

" Mr. Whistler," she said, " two years ago I bought one of your pictures, a beautiful thing, and I have never been able to hang it on my walls. It has been loaned to one exhibition after another. Now, to-day I have my carriage with me, and I would like to take it home with me. I am told it is in your possession."

" Dear lady," returned Whistler, " you ask the impossi-

RECOLLECTIONS AND IMPRESSIONS

ble.   I will send it to you at the earliest practicable moment.
You know,—those last slight touches,—which achieve perfection,—make all things beautiful.''   And so forth and so
forth, to the same effect, and the lady drove off without her
picture.

After she had departed, Whistler commenced to poke
around the studio, and, to the great astonishment of a friend
who had been an involuntary listener to the above conversation, he brought forth a canvas.

''Here it is,'' he said.   ''She was right about one thing,
it *is* beautiful.''   And it *was* beautiful.

''But the impudence of these people,'' he continued,
''who think that because they pay a few paltry hundred
pounds they *own* my pictures.   Why, it merely secures them
the privilege of having them in their houses now and then!
The pictures are *mine!*''

However, this side of Whistler is on record in
the case of "The Baronet *vs.* The Butterfly," as he
called the suit of Sir William Eden to obtain possession of the portrait of Lady Eden.

As the circumstances of this famous case illustrate
Whistler's attitude towards his work, and at the
same time his attitude towards those who tried to
deal commercially with him, they are worth recall-
ing :

In June, 1893, Sir William Eden, a wealthy
English baronet, wrote a letter to Goupil & Co., in
London, asking what Mr. Whistler's price would be
for a small picture of Lady Eden, and he was informed that the price would be about five hundred
guineas.   He replied, stating that he thought the
price too high, and said that he would call and see

Mr. Whistler in Paris. Instead of so doing, he applied to a common friend, who wrote Whistler saying that the portrait "is for a friend of mine, on the one hand, and, on the other hand, you will have to paint a very lovely and very elegant woman, whose portrait you will be delighted to undertake," and "under the circumstances I think you might make very liberal concessions."

The matter of price was always a matter of indifference to Whistler,—*if also* of indifference to the other party,—and when Sir William wrote concerning the price, Whistler replied very cordially in January, 1894, as follows :

"DEAR SIR WILLIAM EDEN : Your letter has only just been handed to me, but this may still, perhaps, reach you in the afternoon. It is quite understood as to the little painting, and I think there can be no difficulty about the sum. The only really interesting point is that I should be able to produce the charming picture which, with the aid of Lady Eden, ought to be expected. Once undertaken, however slight, for me one work is as important as another, and even more so, as Calino said. As for the amount, Moore, I fancy, spoke of one hundred to one hundred and fifty pounds."

The letter is quite characteristic of the artist. His interest was in the possibility of producing a charming picture. The amount he mentioned was less than he ordinarily asked for a water-color sketch, and one-fifth that named by Goupil & Co.

It must be noted that the amount is not fixed by Whistler, but is left at from one hundred to one hundred and fifty pounds, depending of course upon the painter's own feeling regarding his work, and not depending in any sense upon the whim of the baronet.

The portrait went on towards completion. Instead of painting a head, as was originally suggested, Whistler painted a full-length figure seated upon a little sofa, the entire composition being quite as elaborate an interior as if the canvas had been five times the size. The picture was about fourteen to sixteen inches long by five or six inches high, and was such an exquisite bit of the painter's art that a representative of a public gallery, who did not know that it was a commission, offered for it twelve hundred dollars, and higher offers were made.

Sir William Eden did not again refer to the price, although he had many opportunities ; but on February 14, St. Valentine's day, the baronet visited the studio and expressed himself as delighted with the picture. On taking leave, he informed Mr. Whistler that he was about to start for India on a hunting-tour, and, taking an envelope from his pocket, he handed it to the artist. "Here is a valentine for you. Look at it after I have gone. Don't bother about it just now."

When the artist opened his "valentine," he found a check for one hundred guineas,—the minimum amount mentioned in his letter. The baronet had taken it upon himself to fix the price of the picture on the eve of his departure. The "valentine" read as follows :

"4 RUE DE PRESBOURG, PARIS, February 14, 1894.

"DEAR MR. WHISTLER : Herewith your valentine,—cheque value one hundred guineas. The picture will always be of inestimable value to me, and will be handed down as an heirloom as long as heirlooms last.

"I shall always look with pleasure to the painting of it,—and, with thanks, remain

"Yours sincerely,
"WILLIAM EDEN."

To which Whistler immediately replied :

"110 RUE DU BAC, PARIS, February 14.

"MY DEAR SIR WILLIAM : I have your valentine. You really are magnificent, and have scored all round.

"I can only hope that the little picture will prove even slightly worthy of all of us, and I rely on Lady Eden's amiable promise to let me add the few last touches we know of. She has been so courageous and kind all along in doing her part.

"With best wishes again for your journey,
"Very faithfully,
"J. McNEILL WHISTLER."

From the legal point of view Whistler made the mistake of not immediately returning the check for one hundred guineas, and the additional mistake of exhibiting the picture in the Salon of the Champ de Mars in the spring of 1894, as No. 1187, under the title of "Brown and Gold. Portrait of Lady E——."

But ultimately the one hundred guineas were returned, and the baronet brought suit to secure the possession of the picture.

RECOLLECTIONS AND IMPRESSIONS

Whistler would have permitted himself to be drawn-and-quartered before Sir William Eden should have any work of his. He felt, and most justly, that a work which had been begun by him, first, to oblige others, and secondly, as a labor of love, had been placed upon a commercial footing of the lowest level. He felt that there had been no real desire to have one of his pictures on account of its artistic merit, but that there had been an attempt to secure something of commercial value for one-third its market price.

The episode of the "valentine," truly ingeniously devised, completely changed the relations between the parties. He painted out the little portrait, substituted another head, and stood ready to return the hundred guineas and to pay whatever damages the court might award the plaintiff; but under no circumstances should the baronet have the picture.

For the first time in the annals of litigation the question was presented for final determination,—whether an artist could be compelled to deliver work which he claimed was not yet finished to his satisfaction, even though he had received the price. Be it said to the credit of the French tribunal of last resort, that it held broadly that the artist is master and proprietor of his work until such time as it shall please him to deliver it. But that, failing delivery, he must return the price with interest thereon, together with such damages as the sitter may have sustained.

OF JAMES A. McNEILL WHISTLER

The hand of the painter cannot be forced by the importunity of either patient or impatient patron, and no man but the painter himself can say when a painting is sufficiently finished to be delivered.

Except in those few cases where Whistler took such intense dislikes to sitters or purchasers that he would not permit them to have his work under any circumstances, there is no instance where the great painter, in unduly delaying the delivery of a picture, had any intention of depriving the owner of what was rightfully his,—namely, the possession of the picture.

Beyond the right of possession, Whistler did not concede much to the owner. Frequently he challenged the owner's right to exhibit without his sanction, and he was quite inclined to deny to the owner the moral right to sell at speculative prices. He had a poor opinion of those who would buy from the artist to sell later at a profit; he classed them as dealers.

Sitters did not always see things in the same light, and became tired, then impatient, sometimes ugly. Then Whistler would no longer like them, and the sittings would come to an end. If the portrait was unfinished, it was cast aside to remain forever unfinished; if finished, the money would be returned and the portrait kept,—under no circumstances to fall into the hands of a person whom he disliked.

The studio contained many an unfinished portrait, some of them works of great beauty, but of complete indifference to Whistler. He lost all interest in them when he lost interest in the sitters ; and it mattered not to him that he had spent and lost days, and weeks, and months of precious time, nor did it matter to him that his sitters had exhausted themselves with numerous and long seances.

Childless, his paintings were his children, and to part with one was like the parting of mother and child.

In these days, when the selling of pictures has become an essential part of the art of painting, it is difficult for people to comprehend the attitude of a man who really did not like to sell.

"What are pictures painted for, if not to sell?" asks the spirit of the age.

It does not seem quite so obvious that poems are written to sell and that music is composed to sell. Even the "practical man" feels that poems and music ought to be made for something more than to sell, and if they are not, they will be the worse for the narrow end in view ; but paintings and sculpture, they are commercial products to be dealt in accordingly.

When Whistler did part with a picture he had no faculty for getting a high price. His prices were very uncertain. To one person he might ask a round sum, to another small,—just as the mood seized him, the price having no particular relation to the painting.

He never could see why paintings should be sold,

like cloth, by the square yard ; why a large picture should necessarily bring more than a small. To him perfection was perfection, whether large or small.

What justifiable reason is there for the commercial schedule of so much for a head, so much for a half-length, so much for a full-length portrait?

The one may, but does by no means necessarily, take a little more time ; but, then, a painter does not value his work by the day.

A perfect thing is a perfect thing, whether large or small, Whistler would frequently say. In the matter of prices he was obliged to yield somewhat to custom, and ask more for large pictures than for small, but he did so reluctantly and intermittently, with the natural result that dealers, who screen pictures as the plasterer does his gravel, could do nothing with him.

Of late years, with a demand far beyond any possible supply, his prices advanced ; but where a Degas, for instance, would sell for five, ten, or fifteen thousand dollars, a Whistler of incomparably greater beauty would sell for a third or a fifth the amount,— proof of what the co-operation of the dealer can do.

Some years ago he showed a visitor several heads of Italian children, each about ten or twelve, by sixteen or eighteen inches in size. With them was a three-quarter length of one of the children. They were all superb bits of portraiture, and akin to the "Little Rose, Lyme Regis," in the Boston Museum of Fine Arts.

RECOLLECTIONS AND IMPRESSIONS

The visitor was eager to get one or more of the pictures. After considerable pressure, he said :

"I think they ought to be worth six hundred guineas each ; don't you ?"

"And the large one ?" said the visitor.

"Oh, the same. That is no more important than the small."

"Very well. May I have all four ?"

"Dear me ! You don't want them all ?"

"If you will let me have them."

"But—" and then the struggle began, "I must look them over ; they are not quite finished."

"But, surely, these two are finished."

"Yes, I might let those go by-and-bye, but not now."

"Will you send them to me ?"

"Yes, certainly, after I have gone over them again."

"I will leave a check."

"God bless me, no ! You must not do that. It will be time enough to send a check after you receive the little pictures."

Needless to say, the pictures were never received. They had just been finished, and he could not bring himself to part with them. It was not a matter of money at all,—likely as not he sold them later for less,—but it was always next to impossible to get him to part with recent work. If he happened to have on hand a picture five or ten years old, possibly that could be bought and taken away, but anything in which he was interested at the time he would not let go.

In 1894 he exhibited three small marines, which he had painted off-shore while the boatman steadied

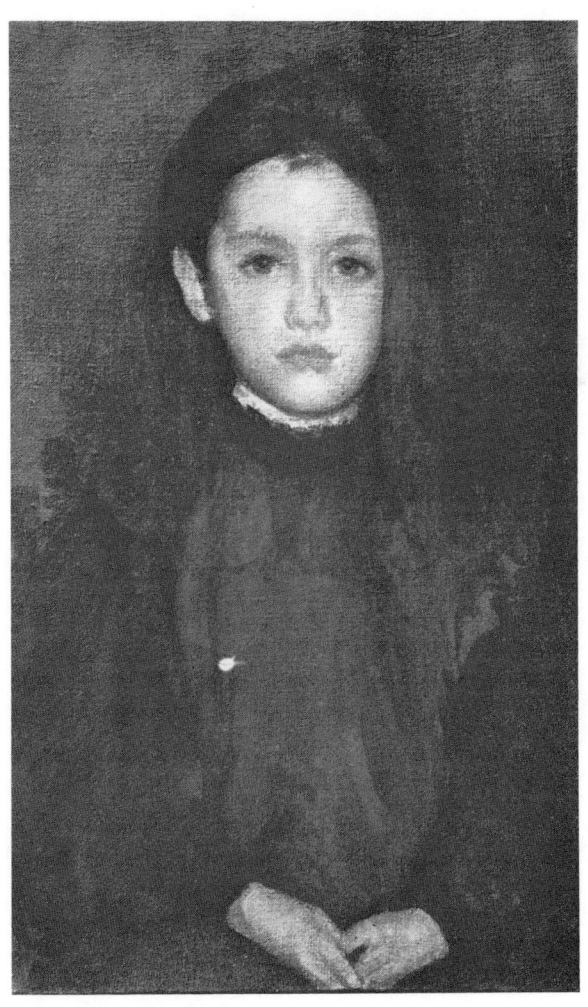

Little Rose, Lyme Regis

his boat. They were fresh and crisp,—so good that a great painter of marines said of them in the exhibition, "They over-topped everything about them."

Two were sold, and he showed the third to an American who came to the studio. The caller said at once he would be only too glad to take it at the price named ; the matter was apparently closed, and the buyer sailed for home, leaving a friend to get the picture.

A day or two after, Whistler stood looking long and earnestly at the little marine, saying half to himself :

" It is good, isn't it ?"

Then he took the canvas out of the frame, and said :

" I think it needs touching up a little."

Another pause, then :

" Do you know, I believe I won't let this go just yet. I want to go over it once more. You know, I can send your friend something else next winter,—something that he may like better. And if he doesn't like it, why, he can return it."

" But, Mr. Whistler, he wants this little marine. There is not much to do upon it, is there ?"

" No—o ; but, then, you see——"

" Well, why not give it the last touches now, and let him have it. If you do not send him this, I am afraid he will never have one of your pictures."

" Oh, yes, he will ; next winter——"

" But next winter others will come in when we are not here, and buy from you whatever you have."

" Well, we will see."

And only persistent urgings, day after day, even after a draft on London had been forced upon him, induced him to ship the painting.

At no time was there any question of price or

money involved; he simply did not wish to part with the last of his three marines.

It was not until about 1890, and after, that Whistler's paintings began to sell at anything like their real worth. To his credit be it said, his work was never "popular."

By his independence, his seeming defiance of all conventional and academic notions in his art, his eccentricities, and his lack of commercial instincts he managed, at a very early period in his career, to alienate,—

Dealers,
Painters, and
Public,

the three factors upon which commercial success depends.

"A millionaire—one who was getting up an art-gallery—went to Whistler's studio and glanced casually at the pictures.

"'How much for the lot?' he asked, with the confidence of one who owns gold mines.

"'Your millions,' said Whistler.

"'What!'

"'My posthumous prices.' And the painter added, 'Good-morning.'"

OF JAMES A. McNEILL WHISTLER

X

*The School of Carmen—In Search of Health—
Chelsea once more—The End.*

To please Madame Carmen Rossi, who as a child
had been one of his best models, Whistler consented in 1897 to criticise the work of such students
as might attend her school.   As a result Carmen's
atelier was for the time being the most distinguished
in Paris, and it was not uncommon to see carriages
with coachmen and footmen in livery before the
door on the days that Whistler was expected.

As he passed about among the pupils he seldom
praised and was never enthusiastic.   He would
sometimes stand many minutes before a canvas that
merited his attention and would suggest changes
and improvements ; and now and then he took a
brush and made the alterations himself, remarking,
if the student were a young woman, " Now you have
a Whistler all to your charming self."

The story is told that once he stopped before a
very brilliant canvas, and exclaimed, " Hideous !
hideous !"   The student said, somewhat proudly,
that she had taken private lessons from Bouguereau,
and he blandly inquired, " Bouguereau, Bouguereau,
—who is Bouguereau ?"

277

RECOLLECTIONS AND IMPRESSIONS

A pupil has printed some reminiscences of those days :[1]

"Usually Mr. Whistler came once a week to criticise us, and on those days the class, numbering anywhere from fifteen to forty, had been instructed to adopt a certain respectful mode of bearing on the arrival of the master ; so, when the concierge threw wide the door and formally announced, 'Monsieur Whistler,' every student had risen to return his ceremonious salutation. Vividly I recall the scene : a man of not much more than medium stature, but so slight as to give the impression, when standing apart from others, of being much taller ; dressed entirely in black, even to the suéde gloves ; every garment immaculate in fit and condition ; a little red rosette of the Legion of Honor of France forming the only spot of color about him until a faint flush rose to his cheek as he greeted the class with kindly smile.

"Then, as *massier* (or monitor, in charge of the class), he passed me his long, black, fur-lined coat and tall, straight-brimmed hat,—those well-known targets for the caricaturist,—and began his criticism by inspecting every drawing and weighing its merits—if any there were, as only too rarely happened—before uttering a word. This silent inspection finished, Mr. Whistler usually asked for a palette,—preferably mine, because it was patterned after his own, and made him 'feel at home,' as he expressed it,—and then, without removing his gloves, painted a few strokes here and there on some of the pupils' work. Even in the matter of a palette he evinced marked sentiment. A carelessly kept one was, above all, his particular abhorrence, and generally elicited some such remark as the following : 'My friends, have you noticed the way in which a musician cares for his violin— how beautiful it is ? how well kept ? how tenderly handled ? Your palette is your instrument, its colors the notes, and upon it you play your symphonies.'

---

[1] E. S. Crawford, in *The Reader*, September, 1903.

"As an instructor he was courteous to each pupil, but naturally most interested in those who followed his precepts closest. Sometimes he jested at the expense of a luckless pupil. I remember an amusing instance. Smoking was prohibited on the days for criticism, since our master believed it clouded the atelier and in some degree obscured a view of the model. One day, upon entering, Mr. Whistler noticed an Englishman, much addicted to his huge cigars, who continued puffing away contentedly during the 'criticism.' Mr. Whistler turned quickly, asking me why his wishes were not enforced ; but before I could frame a reply he had addressed our British friend, saying, 'Er—my dear sir, I know you do not smoke to show disrespect to my request that the students should refrain from smoking on the days I come to them, nor would you desire to infringe upon the rules of the atelier—but—er—it seems to me—er—that when you are painting—er—you might possibly become so absorbed in your work as to—er—well—let your cigar go out.' I often remarked a whimsical affectation of Mr. Whistler in his manner of speech with different pupils in his class,—we were a diverse lot from many lands, Americans and English predominating. If criticising an American, for instance, Mr. Whistler's choice of language, and in some cases his accent, would become markedly English in form ; while in addressing an Englishman he would adopt the Yankee drawl, sometimes adding a touch of local slang. I subsequently learned that these were his customary tactics, even in society, but in class criticism he always addressed us in French."

His methods of teaching were original. He laid little stress on drawing. He hated and despised academic treatment. He wanted the pupil to paint. A few careful charcoal strokes on the canvas as a guide, the rest to be drawn in with brush and color. And he preached simplicity,—as few tones as possible, as low as possible. But it is painful to record that the endeavors of a certain proportion of the class to attempt the achievements of the master in this respect resulted in a unique crop of posters. The constant theme of his discourse was "mixtures." He advised a pupil to get first on his palette a correct and sufficient mixture of each tone required for his picture. Often he would give a long criticism without so much as glancing at the canvas,—a criticism on the mixtures he found on the pupil's palette; and he himself would work indefinitely at the colors, and all the while talking, till it appeared to him to be satisfactory. "And then," says an enthusiastic young artist, "when he did take up some of the color and transfer it to the canvas, why, it would just sing."

"One day on entering the class-room he discovered that a red background had been arranged behind the model. He was horrified, and directed the students to put up something duller in tone.

"Then he scraped out the red paint on a pupil's canvas and proceeded to mix and lay on a new background. Somehow the red would show through, and he found it difficult to satisfy himself with the effect he produced. He mixed and studied and scraped, working laboriously, surrounded by a group of admiring students. Finally, he remarked:

"'I suppose you know what I'm trying to do?'

"'Oh, yes, sir,' they chorused.

"'Well, it's more than I know myself,' he grimly replied."

It is to be hoped that his epigrammatic utterances which hung on the walls of the Carmen Rossi school have been preserved, for they would be valuable additions to the "Propositions" and "Ten o'Clock" already published.

With none of the instincts of the teacher, he in time lost interest in the school. After a year or two his visits became infrequent, and upon leaving Paris his connection ceased.

The studio in Notre Dame des Champs and the home on the Rue du Bac were closed a few years after the death of Mrs. Whistler, and he made his home once more in Chelsea, at 74 Cheyne Walk, with frequent excursions to the Continent.

In the winter of 1901 he was at Ajaccio, and he wrote to a friend : "You will be surprised at this present address.   But it's all right,—" Napoleon and I, you know."

In another letter to the same friend, speaking of a public official with whom he had some legal transactions, he remarks: "Say that I know how devotedly kind he has been in his care of me, but the care of the state overwhelms him.   You cannot serve the republic . . . and Whistler."

For many years his heart had troubled him, and towards the last the warnings came more frequently and persistently.   The year before his death he was quite ill at The Hague, and one of the London papers printed the following of a semi-obituary flavor :

"Mr. Whistler is so young in spirit that his friends

must have read with surprise the Dutch physician's pronouncement that the present illness is due to 'advanced age.' In England sixty-seven is not exactly regarded as 'advanced age ;' but even for the gay 'butterfly' time does not stand still, and some who are unacquainted with the details of Mr. Whistler's career, though they may know his work well, will be surprised to hear that he was exhibiting at the Academy forty-three years ago. His contributions to the exhibition of 1859 were 'Two Etchings from Nature,' and at intervals during the following fourteen or fifteen years Mr. Whistler was represented at the Academy by a number of works, both paintings and etchings. In 1863 his contributions numbered seven in all, and in 1865 four. Among his Academy pictures of 1865 was the famous 'Little White Girl,'[1] the painting that attracted so much attention at the Paris Exhibition of 1900. This picture—rejected at the Salon of 1863—was inspired, though the fact seems to have been forgotten of late, by the following lines of Swinburne :

> " 'Come snow, come wind or thunder
> High up in air,
> I watch my face and wonder
> At my bright hair, etc., etc.' "

The item called forth the following characteristic correction, dated from The Hague :

"SIR : I feel it no indiscretion to speak of my 'convalescence' since you have given it official existence.

---

[1] See page 185.

Symphony in White, No. II.
The Little White Girl

OF JAMES A. McNEILL WHISTLER

"May I therefore acknowledge the tender little glow of health induced by reading, as I sat here in the morning sun, the flattering attention paid me by your gentleman of ready wreath and quick biography.

"I cannot, as I look at my improving self with daily satisfaction, really believe it all; still it has helped to do me good. And it is with almost sorrow that I must beg you, perhaps, to put back into its pigeon-hole, for later on, this present summary, and replace it with something preparatory —which, doubtless, you have also ready.

"This will give you time, moreover, for some correction, —if really it be worth while. But certainly the 'Little White Girl,' which was not rejected at the Salon of '63, was, I am forced to say, not 'inspired by the following lines of Swinburne,' for the one simple reason that those lines were only written, in my studio, after the picture was painted. And the writing of them was a rare and graceful tribute from the poet to the painter—a noble recognition of one work by the production of a nobler one.

"Again, of 'the many tales concerning the hanging, at the Academy, of the well-known portrait of the artist's mother, now at the Luxembourg,' one is true—let us trust your gentleman may have time to find it out—that I may correct it. I surely may always hereafter rely on the *Morning Post* to see that no vulgar Woking joke reach me.

"It is my marvellous privilege, then, to come back, as who should say, while the air is still warm with appreciation, affection, and regret, and to learn in how little I had offended.

"The continuing to wear my own hair and eyebrows, after distinguished confrères and eminent persons had long ceased their habit, has, I gather, clearly given pain. This, I see, is much remarked on. It is even found inconsiderate and unseemly in me, as hinting at affectation.

"I might beg you, sir, to find a pretty place for this, that I would make my 'apology,' containing also promise, in

283

RECOLLECTIONS AND IMPRESSIONS

years to come, to lose these outer signs of vexing presumption.

"Protesting, with full enjoyment of its unmerited eulogy, against your premature tablet, I ask you again to contradict it, and appeal to your own sense of kind sympathy when I tell you I learn that I have, lurking in London, still 'a friend'—though for the life of me I cannot remember his name.

"And I have, sir, the honor to be

"J. McNeill Whistler."

In the spring of 1903, only a few months before his death, three of his pictures were withdrawn from the annual exhibition of the Society of American Artists in New York. They had not been sent in by him, but loaned by the owner upon the understanding they would be given the prominence which he thought Whistler's work deserved.

In the absence of the owner in Europe the whole matter was left in charge of a member of the society, —a well-known artist,—who, when he saw where the committee had placed the little pictures, promptly withdrew them, and notified the owner of his action, which was approved.

Whistler learned of the matter, and wrote the following letter:

"Dear Mr. L——: I have just learned with distress that my canvases have been a trouble and a cause of thought to the gentlemen of the hanging committee.

"Pray present to them my compliments and my deep regrets.

"I fear also that this is not the first time of simple and good-natured intrusion,—'looking in,' as who should say, with beaming fellowship and crass camaraderie upon the highly-finished table and well-seated guests,—to be kindly and swiftly shuffled into some further respectable place, that all be well and hospitality endure.

"Promise, then, for me, that I have learned and that this 'shall not occur again.' And, above all, do not allow a matter of colossal importance to ever interfere with the afternoon habit of peace and good will and the leaf of the mint so pleasantly associated with this society.

"I could not be other than much affected by your warm and immediate demonstration, but I should never forgive myself were the consequences of lasting vexation to your distinguished confrères, and, believe me, dear Mr. L——, very sincerely,

"J. McNEILL WHISTLER.

"LONDON, April 7, 1903."

To the end he worked with indefatigable energy, save only those days and hours when he was compelled by exhaustion or by the physicians to rest.

Work was a tonic to him, and, while painting, the rebellious organs of his body were submissive to his genius.

He would forget himself when, brush in hand, he stood before a canvas.

During the spring of 1903 he had been far from well. Into May he worked, but not regularly nor for long at a time. In June he was quite ill, and his friends were apprehensive ; but in the early part of July he began to gain, so that he took long drives and planned resuming his work.

On the afternoon of July 16 he was out for a drive and in the best of spirits, with plans for the

future that even a younger man could not hope to
execute.

Art, the ever-youthful mistress of his life, urged
him on. Should he confess before her the ravages
of years? In dauntless enthusiasm, in boundless
ambition, in spirit unsubdued he was still young. He
struggled to his feet and for the last time stood before the canvas,—the magic mirror from which he,
wizzard-like, had evoked so many beautiful images ;
he thought of the things he yet would do, of lines
that would charm for all time, of colors that would
play like the iridescent hues upon the surface of the
shimmering sea, of the wraith-like images of people
which lurked in the depths of the canvas awaiting
the touch of his wand to step forth in all their stately
dignity and beauty.

And the soul of the master was filled with
delight.

> But the visions of beauty were shattered,
> Like forms of the mist they were scattered—
> As bubbles are blown by a breath—
> By the grim, haunting spectre of Death.

The tired body could not respond, and there
where he had worked, on the afternoon of Friday,
July 17, the great painter died.

On the following Wednesday the funeral services
were held in the old church at Chelsea where he
often went with his mother, and he was buried beside her in the graveyard at Chiswick.

"*We have then but to wait—until with the mark of the gods upon him—there come among us again the chosen—who shall continue what has gone before. Satisfied that, even were he never to appear, the story of the beautiful is already complete—hewn in the marbles of the Parthenon—and broidered, with the birds, upon the fan of Hokusai—at the foot of Fusiyama.*"—WHISTLER'S "Ten o'Clock."

INDEX

Ajaccio, 281

Albany, 33

Allen, Sir William, 35

America, attitude towards, 52–53; desire to visit, 22; trip to South America, 22–23

American appreciation, 15–17; art, future of, 63–64; characteristics, 64–65

Americanism, Whistler's, 47–48

Ancestors, 25–28

Anecdotes and sayings, as a teacher, 277–281; attitude towards America, 52–53; authenticity of stories, 81–82; bailiff in the "White House," 112–113; Balaam's ass, 84–85; blue-and-white china, 70; Boer war, 45; Carlyle portrait, 123; colors and pigments used, 72–73; concerning a sitter, 238–239; concerning birth, 29; concerning Carlyle and Miss Alexander, 121; concerning Chicago, 27; concerning each portrait, 241–242; concerning his portraits, 255; concerning poor lawyers, 148; concerning purchasers, 265–266; concerning sittings required, 30–31; continually polishing, 84–85; Dieppe, 34; disintegration of the Royal Society of British Artists, 218; early days in Paris, 86–88; early days in Venice, 92–95; effacing an insult, 43; falling down stairs, 114; first money earned with brush, 80–81; Henry James, 85; his umbrella, 227; Hogarth, 55; house-painters, 212; late to dinner, 29–30; Leighton, 82–84; in lithography suit, 103; man whose coat did not fit, 42; "Nana," 151–153; Napoleon and I, 281; Nature looking up, 214; necktie of a sitter, 191; no artistic period, 73–78; old Delft, 71; painting in the dark, 214; "Peacock Room," 129; of Peter the Great, 35; railway accident, 33–34; rebuking an admirer, 162; rich man's house, 56; Rossetti, 111; Royal Academy, 116–119; Savoy Hotel, 181; school, 61; selling his pictures, 274–275; Stoeckl dinner,

INDEX

INDEX

INDEX

cism of Turner, 142–143; George Moore, 168–172; his attitude towards, 155–157; his color harmonies not understood, 184; is the painter the final judge? 162–165; order of appreciation, 173–175; Ruskin's attitude towards color, 158–160; "Voice of a People," 165–167

Dealers, attitude towards, 276

Death and last illness, 285–286

Decoration, 127–133; as a decorator, 131–135; in home in Paris, 220–222; "Peacock Room," 128–131, 209

Dieppe, 33–34

Dress, 41–42

Eden, Sir William, 267–270

England's indifference, 47–49

Englishman's stupidity, 16

Etchings, appreciation of a collector, 96–97; of Haden, 96; catalogues of, 91; early French criticism, 60; "French Set," 90; Haden collection of, 96; his first, 88–89; his "Venice Set," 91; "Thames Set," 91; "Twenty-six Etchings," 91

Exhibitions, 1868, 177; 1893, 65; at Antwerp, 263; at Chicago, 263; at London, 265; at Paris, 1894, 24, 264; at the Royal Academy, 114–119; criticisms of, 98–101; his catalogues, 99–101; light and background required for his pictures, 134–139; of etchings, 1883, 97; of lithographs, 104; reluctant about exhibiting, 262–264; Society of American Artists in 1903, 284–285; Society of British Artists, 136; special, 120–121; with artificial light, 135; "Yellow and White," 98, 132

Family, 25–28; brothers and sisters, 32; father, 27–28, 35; mother, 28; mother's diary, 34–35

Fine Arts Society, 121

Foreword, 7

Form, appreciation of, 203

Fort Dearborn, grandfather built, 26–27

French art, influence of, 57–60; criticism, early, 59–60

Frith, 177; Ruskin trial, 146

Fur Jacket," "The, 65

Gainesborough, 249, 250

Gentle Art of Making Enemies," "The, 32, 154–155

Glasgow and the Carlyle portrait, 124; school, 55

INDEX

INDEX

INDEX

INDEX

THE END